MY WARRIOR
AMONG THE SAMBURU OF NORTHERN KENYA

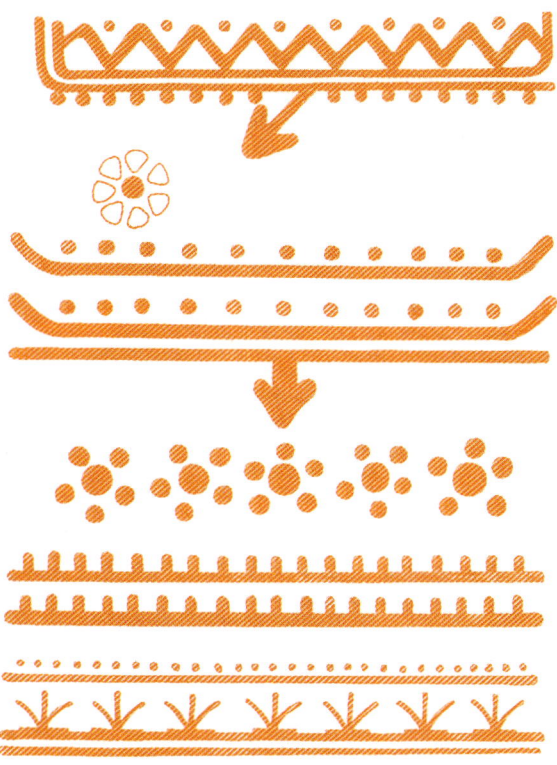

Above: Karaito between circumcision and warriorhood

Overleaf: Samburu face paintings

ROGER STOAKLEY

My Warriors and I

Among the Samburu of Northern Kenya

To Gavin, with best wishes from Roger.

Scriptmate Editions
1998

First published in 1998
by Scriptmate Editions
20 Shepherds Hill
London N6 5AH

Copyright © Roger Stoakley 1998

ISBN 0 9513766 9 1

A catalogue record for this book is available from
the British Library

Roger Stoakley's right to be identified as the author of this
work has been asserted by him in accordance with the
Copyright, Designs and Patents Act 1988.

All rights reserved. No part of this book may be reproduced or
transmitted in any form, electronic or mechanical, including
photocopy or any information storage and retrieval system,
without permission in writing from the publisher.

Typeset in New Century 11/14pt
Manufacture coordinated in UK by
Book-in-Hand Ltd, 20 Shepherds Hill,
London N6 5AH

for Ambrose

Acknowledgements

Levy and Frida Wamanga who have done so much to foster national and international friendships between young people.

Brian and Penny Brown and Dr EZ Hazarika for the compassion they expended on Lturungen.

The headteachers of Somerset who so warmly welcomed Lturungen to their schools.

Stephen Jones, Helen and Stephen Elliot, David Williams and all those others who have supported Lturungen and his people.

My wife Aase Marie for her understanding and encouragement.

Kari, Helena, Frances and Rosemary for the equanimity with which they have accepted so many foreign guests to our home.

Lturungen for all he has taught me about his people and their culture.

Lpiritian for persuading the Elders to allow me to live with the Samburu and to attend their ceremonies.

Ann Kritzinger for editing the text.

Julia Harvey who typed the manuscript.

Photographs and illustrations by the author

Contents

INTRODUCTION	9
CHAPTER ONE Morning — Siran	11
CHAPTER TWO Lturungen	17
CHAPTER THREE England	34
CHAPTER FOUR London	55
CHAPTER FIVE Facing the Elders	63
CHAPTER SIX Water — Nkare	75
CHAPTER SEVEN Night — Nguariye	89
CHAPTER EIGHT Safari	108
CHAPTER NINE Living the Samburu Way	127
CHAPTER TEN Circumcision — Muratare	142

CHAPTER ELEVEN
    Warrior-making: the Ceremony
    of Arrows — Lmuget Loolbaa
	157

CHAPTER TWELVE Archer's Post	172
CHAPTER THIRTEEN Farewell — Lesere	191
LIST OF CHARACTERS	197
GLOSSARY	199

Introduction

The involvement of two of our daughters in an internationally based musical about world peace, led to us acting as hosts to two young Kenyans, one from the Digo tribe on the coast and the other from the belligerent and nomadic Pokot close to the Ugandan border. The boys lived with us for almost two months, and despite our disparate backgrounds and cultures, we were surprised how well they fitted into the family.

When they returned home, my wife and I followed them and were looked after by one of their schoolteachers. This began a close association with Kenya and the Samburu tribe, one of the last remaining warrior peoples of Africa. They occupy the parched lands of the former Northern Frontier District, the scene of tribal warfare and still subject to tight security. Fiercely independent, and scornful of Western-style living, these semi-nomadic pastoralists have remained relatively untouched by civilisation and are consequently less well known than their cousins, the Maasai.

The 100,000-strong tribe lives in an area of roughly 8000 square miles just north of the equator, and is divided into eight clans. It has a well-ordered social structure based on age-sets.

There are many rituals, the two most important being circumcision and warrior-making. The tribe has no rulers — law and order being maintained by the senior elders who use the power of the curse as the ultimate sanction.

The activities of the Samburu — and their very survival — are governed by the availability of water and grazing and the well-being of their cattle to which they have a strong emotional attachment. The size of a man's herd reflects his social standing, including the number of wives he has, and his cattle provide him with his basic food and commodities.

Although several books of photographs have been published which describe Samburu customs and ceremonies, it is unusual for an outsider to have lived with them for any length of time, or to have been adopted as a member of a family. This was a privilege granted to me shortly before the close of the four-year period of circumcision and warrior-making ceremonies in 1994, on condition that I conformed to their lifestyle. The opportunity gave me a detailed insight into their way of living, their beliefs, their fears and their outlook on life.

The experience was enriched through a close association with one of their number — a cripple — who prior to this event came to live with us in England for the three months while he underwent an operation on his foot. During that time I learned a great deal about Samburu tribal customs and traditions, and his reaction to our contrasting way of life provided a unique opportunity to study the thought patterns and attitudes of his people. I was left with the overall impression that communities who still live close to nature have much to teach us.

The strength of the Samburu lies in their remarkable self-confidence and their ability to change and adapt. Theirs is a living tradition, and so long as future governments do not take away their lands from them I believe their way of life will survive well into the next century.

CHAPTER ONE

Morning — *Siran*

woman's bead decoration

THE SOFT GREY LIGHT of predawn crept in through the window — a few vertical sticks like window bars within a frame of woven twigs and branches. I could just see the outline of cattle, some standing, some lying, and all of them motionless as if transfixed by the first glimmer of light. It was, as the Africans say, the time when the earth and the sky separate.

I turned on my back and looked up. Four foot above was the same woven structure of twigs and branches. They were held in place by longer pliable rods which ran in great arcs across the ceiling and down the walls, with a sturdy stave supporting the roof near its centre. There was a door that was so low and so narrow that you could, with difficulty, just squeeze through it bent double. Rounded at both ends, this little shelter was for all the world like an upturned basket with a roof of mud and dung as insulation against the noonday heat and the rains, if ever they came. A nomadic home, this entire abode could be easily dismantled and built again in a new location in half a day.

Everything was quite still. I felt at ease. For a moment I drifted back into a half-dream state, into a feeling of immense freedom. I was at home, and yet I was not at home. I put my hand out and felt around. The bed was not a familiar raised rectangle with its four edges. It was a few branches placed on the ground. The mattress was a cow hide, and the bedding was the same simple strip of cloth that covered my otherwise naked body during the day.

"For dust thou art and unto dust shalt thou return." There was dust enough around; dust that had not been dampened by rain for six months or more. It was pervasive. It filled your shoes. It crept up your legs. It clogged your nose. It lay in miniature drifts in the creases of your ears. It made your hair stiff and starchy. Spurts of dust rose from your heels with every step and, when the cattle were on the move, great clouds of dust filled the air, rolling over huts and trees and people like a great sea mist. I could feel it now on the cow hide, dry, powdery, fine red dust. Trapped under the cow hide, dust had afforded me a night's sleep.

That selfsame dust compacted as earth gave anchorage to what little grass was left for the cattle to feed on. It secured and nourished the trees and bushes on whose leaves and twigs the camels and goats browsed. The animals in their turn provided the milk, the blood and the meat which enabled the tribesmen to grow, mature and procreate until through age or sickness, or perhaps mishap, they returned in death to the earth. Here a child is born on the ground, just as an animal is born, and when life is over the body is laid out on the ground and covered with twigs and left in just the same way as the carcasses of animals are left, their dried and bleached bones their only tombstone.

Slowly the rim of the sun appeared over the distant mountains. There is no dawn chorus here. The few brightly coloured birds which survived the drought and the blunted arrows of the newly circumcised boys, sought the shelter of distant trees, and the occasional vulture which wheeled overhead ever-watchful for carrion, did not have a melodious voice.

As the sun climbed above the horizon, the grey was transformed into the palest rose-pink. Instantly, everything these first rays touched took on the same hue, the cattle, the soil, the scattered trees and the huts as they emerged in the fanfare of light. And still there was silence and no movement.

In the gathering light I could see the outline of four slumbering bodies between myself and the window. The one furthest away was that of a boy of about eleven or twelve. His name was Karaito. Of the three brothers sharing this home he was the youngest. Then there was a small child, Alberto, not yet two years old. He was full of cold and sorely vexed; his eyes had streamed all the previous day and he had suffered a restless night. Now fast asleep, he lay on his back completely naked. Next to him lay Lpiritian his father, the eldest of the brothers. He was snoring and his arm cradled his head as he lay on his side. Nearest to me was the long low profile of Lturungen, the third brother. He was swathed in cloth so completely that you could not tell for certain which end was his head and which end were his feet.

My attention centred on Lpiritian and Lturungen. Had Adam lain like this, I wondered, when he adopted a human frame and was turned out of the Garden of Eden? And did he, like these two, resort to a simple robe of skin or cloth to hide his nakedness? Civilisation deludes us into believing that only civilisation engenders the finer human qualities, the finest of which I had detected in the two companions lying nearest me. Civilisation upon civilisation had, like sparks in the night sky, risen to its zenith, glowed for a while with all its complexity of laws and culture, its conquering and clamouring, wielding of power, its pomp and splendour, and then dimmed and faded. All had passed these Samburu by — people who live as men must have lived at the beginning of the human race.

There was the familiar sound of snapping firewood. Then the fire which lay between ourselves and the door was stirred into life. The wood crackled as it burned; like everything else around it was tinder-dry and created very little smoke. As the flames shot upwards they revealed the figure of a woman. Her face had strong features and her bearing was one of quiet confidence. But although she was barely forty years old, her eyelids were sunken, and the rigours of the climate had lined her forehead and parched her skin. Her hair was close-cropped; round her waist she wore a faded blue skirt. Necklaces of small beads — predominantly red, but with some blue and yellow and green — covered her from the neck to the mid-point of her chest, partly obscuring two pendulous breasts. Round her arms she wore bangles. The tops of her ears had been pierced, and from each of them there sprouted a curved spike of wire-mounted beads, looking for all the world like two small antennae. Her earlobes too had been pierced, and stretched so much with earrings that they hung in a sinuous loop some two or three inches long.

She had spent the night in her own compartment on the right of the doorway while an elderly female companion occupied the compartment on the left. Now she was sitting in front of the fire. Nearly four years a widow, she had been the second of four wives. Samburu men marry late — it is they who pay a dowry of cattle to the wife's family, and they may also take more than one wife if they have sufficient cattle to meet the dowry payments. The girls marry early, and this woman's late husband had been more than twice her age when he died. She had had one daughter and six sons. One had drowned in tragic circumstances just before his circumcision and the other had been killed by Somali bandits raiding the village. Now one son had stayed at home to look after the livestock and the women of the family, and the other three sons had come to the *lorora* for the circumcision ceremonies in which Karaito, her youngest son had taken part.

The two months this woman was spending in the *lorora* would mark a significant change in her life. Within a few days Karaito would be made a warrior of the tribe in a splendid day of feasting and dancing, at the end of which he would sever his childhood links with his mother for ever. For the next ten years or so, he would roam freely in the company of his age-mates. From the time he became a warrior his mother would be subservient to him and obliged to carry out his every wish. In losing the last of her sons, she hoped instead to gain a grandson to nurture through childhood, and I saw her looking longingly at little Alberto asleep on the floor.

Unlike her sons the woman had few words and little laughter, but when she did speak she spoke earnestly and with a decisiveness which, in common with the features of her face, revealed a great strength of character.

Staying at the *lorora* at the behest of her sons, she had no option but to accept me as a guest. In her society the men command, the women serve. Even so, I never ceased to be amazed at the equanimity with which she received me into the family. As far as I could establish, no white man had lived with the Samburu in these parts. She had never spoken to a *mzungu* before and still less shaken hands with one. Her attitude was one of indifference, but insomuch as this indifference was directed at everyone, whether it be son, daughter, step-children or the other wives, I was made welcome as if I had been a relative.

The water in the cooking pot was now on the point of boiling. Goats milk, tea and sugar were poured into the water from a calabash and other containers which had been hanging on the wall of her compartment. Then, because there were no spoons with which to stir the contents, there began the curious business of pouring the mixture from one cooking pot to another and back again several times to dissolve the sugar and brew the tea. This soothing swish swish of liquid is one of the first sounds a Samburu child hears on waking each morning. It seemed to me it must be one of two sounds that they would carry with them for the rest of their lives. The other is the hollow clackety-clack of the milk gourds as they are cleaned out daily with a swab fashioned from a cow's tail mounted on a wooden handle.

When the tea was ready it was poured into chipped enamel mugs and a mug was placed at our feet. It was the signal to get up. By the window Karaito sat rocking backwards and forwards with his arms clasped round his legs waiting for his tea to cool. Now, nearly a month after his circumcision, he had only recently reverted to his bed on the ground in place of the raised cot which he used while his wounds healed. Lpiritian, who had become head of the family after the death of his father, propped himself up on one arm and sipped his tea thoughtfully, while

Lturungen emerged from his shroud-like cocoon. Both he and I deftly, and with decorum, transformed the sheets which had covered us in the night back into our daytime garments. When we had drunk our tea and put on our shoes we each of us got up and, carefully skirting the fire, went through the door and out into the morning air.

CHAPTER TWO

Lturungen

Samburu headrest

I WAS SUFFERING from culture shock. I was in the bush, wearing only a *nanga*, and devoid of most of the belongings on which I was normally dependent. There were a few exceptions — a camera, tape recorder, razor and malaria and water sterilisation tablets, packed into a small rucksack. We were on our way to the *lorora* — a ceremonial encampment specially constructed for the circumcision of boys.

I had only a vague recollection of the way we had come and no idea of where we were going. It was a desolate area of drought-stricken trees and bushes. Green was a luxury in these parts reserved only for a few fleshy plants and the crowns of trees. All else was bleached grey by a merciless sun. Flies buzzed menacingly around our heads as we journeyed, and the sandy soil was hot to the feet, even through shoes. I wondered how Lpiritian and Lturungen found their way about here. The brothers walked ahead navigating by the landmarks they knew, but which I could not pick out with my untrained eye.

We passed a couple of settlements tucked behind the trees without my being aware of them. The boys laughed and made fun of me when I said I hadn't seen them. The brown of the mud and the wickerwork merged with the dried branches of the thorn fences surrounding them, and the fences themselves were virtually indistinguishable from the rain-starved furze of scrub which grew on every side. I felt apprehensive and vulnerable.

We had set out on this safari without our spears and this was another cause for alarm. We had no protection against wild animals. The boys were in unusually high spirits. "There are no dangerous animals round here," they grinned in assurance. "And if we do meet some we will just shin up the nearest tree."

That was all very well for them, I thought. They were young and agile, but my elderly joints would not relish taking flight up into the safety of branches. Most of these trees were acacias with two-inch long thorns. Seeking protection in one of those would be about as comfortable as hiding in a coil of barbed wire. The prospect was hardly more appealing than the risk of being mauled by a lion or charged by a buffalo.

The ground was undulating and as we walked our feet sank into soft sand. Our route led across a dried river bed. We sat for a while on a bank under the scant shade of near leafless trees. Lturungen walked down to a stagnant pool, pulled aside the thorn branches surrounding it, knelt down and scooped up the dark water in his hands and drank. I shuddered.

As I sat there my mind went back three years to the shade of other trees, standing with my wife on a bluff not very many miles from where I was now. Below us the Wuaso Ngiro — the 'Brown River' — was running fast.

Little eddies of current encircled the rocks, yet it had the dullness of brown soup despite the brightness of the sun, for it was opaque with mud. The river is an artery in an otherwise parched land. The Samburu could not survive on these plains without it.

"Nkai gave us the river for our own needs," Lpiritian maintained.

Looking down from the mountains, the river is reminiscent of a snake twisting and slithering across the earth from west to east. It marks a physical and cultural boundary — is the divide between the settled lands to the south and the great untamed territory of the former Northern Frontier District. Cross the river from the south, and the whole of the Samburu plain opens up before you. Its dimensions are vast: formed of stony steppe relieved by clumps of trees and thorny scrubland, dried river beds and rocky outcrops, it is dominated from this vantage point by the massive table mountain of Ol doinyo Sabachi. The diminutive Samburu encampments make no impression on the landscape; made from natural vegetation they merge into their surroundings so perfectly that they are invisible to the eye. Superficially this land gives the appearance of being devoid of human life, and you could be forgiven for thinking you had reached the end of the earth.

Across the river that day our attention was caught by the glint of sunlight on metal. Moments later, three near-naked young men emerged from the trees. Each one carried a spear, a club-like stick and a short sword. These Samburu warriors, or *lmurran* as they are known, sat on a rock by the water's edge and then, after some moments of discussion prepared to ford the river.

They stripped off their loincloths and held them high in their left hands while they proceeded to cross the shallowest part at a leisurely pace. Holding their spears in their right hands, they used them blade-uppermost and pointed end down, in much the same way as a blind man uses a stick to tap his way along the street.

At the time we were mystified by the procedure, but later it was a technique I learned for myself. It isn't done to save yourself the embarrassment and pain of stubbing your toe against a submerged rock. You do it to avoid stepping on a crocodile! Sometimes you would see them lying just below the surface, two eyes and a snout protruding above the water, or sunning themselves on the bank, but in the main they prefer the deeper stretches so it is only logical to choose the shallowest places to cross. Even then a crocodile may be lurking in a gully ready to catch the unwary. Tap one on the head with the point of your spear as you feel your way across the river and your impudence enrages him. A thrashing tail and churning water is the signal to step smartly backwards and beyond the reach of snapping jaws if you don't want to end up as someone else's lunch.

Once across the river, the warriors replaced their clothing and sauntered towards us. It was our first encounter with Samburu warriors. These slender elegant people, their lithe and graceful bodies, their stature and their grave and simple demeanour were at one and the same time proud, glorious, vain, brave and carefree.

In some ways the tribe understands the needs of young men better than we do. These warriors of northern Kenya live an idyllic life, freed of direct family ties, shielded by distance from ministerial edicts forbidding cattle rustling and the hunting of lions, adored by the young girls of the tribe with whom they are allowed to satisfy their sexual desires, and responsible only for the defence of their communities and their cattle from marauding animals and hostile neighbours. It is the ideal way of allowing them to let off steam, indulge in the exuberance of youth and prove their manliness before settling down to the sober activities of married life.

Released from the duties and restraints of childhood, they celebrate their freedom with a liberal application of red ochre to their hair, face, neck and upper chest, and adopt a bizarre hairstyle. First treated with a mixture of ash and cow urine to make it supple, their hair is plaited into long strands which grow down at the back of the head to below the shoulder blades. There is a parting from ear to ear, and the remaining hair is plaited and pulled forward to create either a fringe above the eyebrows held in place by strings of beads and large mother-of-pearl buttons, or held together to protrude some inches in front of the forehead like a sunshade.

Their hairstyle is their pre-occupation. The hair is constantly groomed using a little wooden spatula. When they sleep they use a headrest in place of a pillow so that their coiffure is not damaged, and when they dance they tie a piece of cloth round their hair and under their chin so that none of the plaited strands should fall out of place.

Plugs of ivory decorate their earlobes; strings of coloured beads adorn their necks and arms, and they wear cuffs of beads around their wrists. Their vanity knows no bounds, and is rivalled only by that of the Maasai. Give a warrior a mirror — a rare and valuable commodity in these parts — and he is your friend for life.

The spears they carry protect them from both wild animals and Somali bandits from the east. The razor-sharp oval blade can pierce a man at twenty yards or more, and the warriors learn to throw their weapons with deadly accuracy.

We felt a little vulnerable as they approached; would they be hostile or friendly? Fear of attack by human predators has always been the curse of African life and the history of East Africa is written in blood, tribe massacring tribe, and since the arrival of the white man, Africans killing Europeans and Europeans shooting Africans. Under British rule the Northern Frontier District was notorious for its tribal conflicts, and latterly the Somali Shifta have added to the blood spilt on Kenyan soil. Neither have the Samburu themselves been exempt from internecine warfare. They have an unenviable reputation for killing cold-bloodedly during cattle raids.

Now the emergence of an urban culture in Kenya has brought inter-tribal conflict to the towns and cities where its pursuit is more subtle. Instead of outright murder, tribal feuds emerge in the form of muggings, break-ins, harassment and rape.

Our misgivings were unfounded. As they passed, each of the faces broke into a broad grin. We were on friendly terms. This had been our first visit to Kenya, and we had by chance already met Lpiritian. I could never have imagined then that within the space of a couple of years, and drawn together to witness the circumcision of Lpiritian's youngest brother Karaito and half brother Lobuka, I and these young men would become the best of friends.

Lturungen finished drinking, replaced the thorn branches, and we continued on our way. We arrived at the *lorora* without mishap. This was an encampment of a size I could not possibly have missed. Here were a dozen or more huts and a medley of children, elders and women. There were also warriors in their finery. We stopped outside the hut occupied by the mother of Lpiritian and Lturungen. People gathered round and I was introduced and offered a mug of tea.

When we came to know Lpiritian, his father's death at the age of eighty four had coincided with the worst of the drought, and his herds had dwindled to just a few animals on the edge of starvation. The eldest son of the second of four wives and barely out of his teens, Lpiritian was pitched into a position of responsibility both for his family and the family of the third wife who lived with them. With insufficient food to feed his dependents, he was obliged to undertake menial tasks at a distant tourist lodge, living there in unfamiliar surroundings and separated from his family for weeks at a time. It was there that we befriended him.

Looking at him now enjoying his annual leave, relaxed and happy to be back in familiar surroundings, he seemed a different person from when we had first met him. At the lodge he was an outsider, one of five or six Samburu working there and entertaining the visitors with displays of tribal dancing in the evenings. The permanent staff, the managers, receptionists, cooks, waiters and housekeepers, each trained in their particular roles and drawn from the more prosperous Kenyan tribes scoffed at these uneducated yokels and their rudimentary lifestyle. The lodge had been built on their traditional grazing lands, and yet they were regarded as outsiders and flaunted in front of visitors as quaint throwbacks to the primitive beginnings of mankind.

Lpiritian never mentioned his family in the rather disjointed letters he sent us after we first met him. His English was extremely limited, and reading and writing were skills he had never mastered. Communication was for him an arduous task helped only by the fact that he had a good spoken knowledge of Swahili, the lingua franca of East Africa. When he wanted to correspond he had to seek out somebody who not only spoke his own language or Swahili, but also could translate and write in English. People with these abilities were few and far between, and when letters did arrive the language was stilted and the concepts wooden. I realised they must have been a far cry from the sentiments he would wish to have expressed, and I wondered what impression my letters left with him when they had been read and translated by a foreign eye.

Then one day a letter arrived in splendid English, full of expression and feeling, and signed not only by Lpiritian but also Lturungen. Lturungen explained that he was a younger brother attending secondary school on the slopes of Mount Kenya, and that he would write on Lpiritian's behalf when he was home from his studies. The correspondence continued. Lturungen obviously loved writing and his colourful letters vividly portrayed his final year at school and his return home.

In time we came to regard him as a close friend, simply through the strength of personality he conveyed to us through the written word. Each letter presented a new aspect of his character and a fresh slant on his background. Then what had been a cheerful and ebullient correspondence declined into letters of despair. Some of his worries were related to his inability to make use of his education in obtaining a job, but underlying it all was the fact that he was not welcome at home.

He was clearly in serious difficulty and seemed to be looking to us for help. Another trip to Kenya had been planned, but it was already packed full with appointments. There was no time to visit the north. Could we perhaps persuade him to come to Nairobi? The thought of the trauma he might experience as a result of journeying from nomadic isolation to a teeming, throbbing, restless city, the biggest between Cairo and Johannesburg, filled us with misgiving. In the end our minds were made up for us. Friends in Nairobi invited him to stay with them.

In Britain such an invitation would not seem unusual, but in Kenya where life divides along tribal lines it was a challenging and courageous step to take. National borders imposed by colonial powers sitting round negotiating tables in Europe at the turn of the century had more to do with politics and economic gain than ethnic interests. After centuries of freedom of movement, forty or more diverse tribes suddenly found themselves boxed in by boundaries imposed by white men, the boundaries of present-day Kenya. The cultural differences between our Bantu Luyha friends in Nairobi whose roots were near Kimilili in the west, and the Nilo-Hamitic Samburu from the north could hardly have been greater. To invite Lturungen to stay with them was akin to an English family offering hospitality to a stranger from the Orient.

It was arranged that Lturungen would meet us after our arrival in the capital. We were acutely aware of the tribal cultural differences involved, and wanted to smooth out the relationship between him and our friends who were hosting him. However his impulsiveness got the better of him and to our amazement, and the consternation of his hosts, he arrived in advance. It had been a long journey involving much walking and two bus journeys. We wondered how, in such new and strange surroundings, he had managed to find his way to where our friends lived on the extreme outskirts of the city. It seemed that when he spilled out of the overcrowded coach at the Akamba bus station in downtown Nairobi luck was on his side. Almost the first person he stumbled across in the rush and tumble of people was one of his ex-school teachers who recognised him as a former pupil and who obligingly put him on the appropriate local bus.

We always receive such a delightfully warm welcome at our destination in Nairobi. On this occasion the whole family — mother, father, the three sons, Kenny, Allan and Oliver, and Tuta the daughter, were all waiting on the verandah to greet us. Formal handshakes dissolved into the pleasurable informality of hugs and kisses, laughter at the happiness of being together again and the inevitable exclamations of surprise at the way the children had grown since we last saw them. It was a joyous event.

Silent and reserved at the end of the line, feeling utterly excluded from this reunion, stood Lturungen. The Nairobi family's elated greetings were far removed from the reserved and circumspect salutations practised by his own tribe. I got the impression that he felt our familiarity with his hosts distanced him from us. Neither was he entirely comfortable in these urban surroundings. It was a new and unfamiliar concept of living for him.

This was the first time he had stayed with a family other than his own, and this family's urban approach to life was disconcerting to him. It was also the first time he had lived in a house. The food he was given was unfamiliar and included vegetables which he found as unpalatable as we might find blood. He was dressed in an ageing T-shirt and an old pair of trousers left over from his schooldays. For him these clothes were ostensibly the badge of a town-dweller. He feared they conferred on him a competence which he did not possess, and which he could not emulate.

Despite their young age, the children of this family were bright. All of them attended private schools. They were the product of an emerging Third World state still suffering the birth pangs of independence and the void left behind by the withdrawal of colonial power. The parents had been the first generation to move out of the village, crossing the mighty gulf that lies between tribal life and the life of the city dweller. Their native prudence and wisdom and their inborn academic abilities enabled them to bridge the divide with relative ease. Now piped water and modern sanitation, rather than spring water and an earth closet, were the norm, and the car had taken the place of the oxcart.

The parents had decided that their children should reflect the idealism of the new Kenya. English was their first language and Swahili the second. Sadly their mother tongue came a poor third. Nevertheless their parents were sickened by the corruption and immorality which is inevitable in a city which attracts so many poor people from the rural areas in search of almost non-existent work, and where tribal values are replaced by the dubious norms of twentieth-century living. So they had brought up their offspring to conform to the standards of behaviour which reflected more of their native background than the culture of present-day Nairobi, and the benefits and discipline of this upbringing were obvious. Nevertheless, living in a large city had its advantages.

The children knew the rudiments of politics and finance; they had a lively interest in world affairs; they were articulate and sharp-witted; all were accomplished at sport. Lturungen found their streetwise urbanity intimidating, and despite his innate composure it nevertheless reinforced his feeling of isolation and cast him in the role of a country bumpkin. Although the family was disciplined, it did not conform to the discipline of Samburu life which had both shaped and governed Lturungen's relationship with others. The Samburu hierarchical system did not apply here, so how should he relate to the children? How should he regard their mother and father? Was he the equivalent of a junior elder in their sight, or should he respond to the parents as if he were a senior elder? Was he to treat the offspring as if they were children, or should he consider them as equivalent to the warrior age-set? The whole business was both worrying and puzzling to him.

Then there was another problem. He had to live down the notion commonly held in Nairobi that those living north of the Wuaso Ngiro were wild and ungovernable. At the same time he had to overcome in his own mind his tribe's conviction that Nairobi was a dangerous and lawless city in which to live, where discipline and moral fibre were beyond redemption.

When I first met Lpiritian I asked him whether he had ever been to the capital. He turned my question over in his mind for a moment, and then "Do you know," he said in a tone of voice which implied I had overlooked something essential, "in Nairobi they kill each other with cars? Here we use our spears and then only to kill our enemies or the lions which attack our cattle."

He had not been there, nor did he want to go there.

There was little chance to talk to Lturungen in those first few busy days. He was taciturn in the extreme. Although he said little I sensed he was thinking and observing much, and above all wondering why fate had brought him to live side by side with people from two cultures so different from his own. Until lately he had come across in his letters as a strong character, a joyful happy-go-lucky fellow full of humour. We had not anticipated the reserve he now exhibited. Was he still in the grip of depression, or was he simply overawed by the situation? We noticed too that he walked with a limp.

At last there came a time when he and I sat in that suburban garden under the spreading branches of an avocado tree amid the flowers and shrubs, and in the delectable warmth of a Nairobi afternoon with the prospect of nothing more than spending a few hours in each other's company.

He began by saying he wanted to show me his foot. I was surprised; I wondered why it was so important. It was not the opening I expected. Neither was I prepared for what he was about to reveal.

Off came the right shoe, followed by the sock, and there in front of me was the burnt remains of what had once been a foot. In fact it was so mutilated that it was little more than a stub — brown, shrivelled and disfigured. Then his story spilled out. Indeed 'spill' is too mild a word. It was as if a dam had burst. Years of anguish, pent-up feeling and pain poured out from him in a flood of words. He talked as if no one had listened to him before — a deluge of emotion delivered with an intensity which tugged at my heartstrings.

I became so involved with his revelations that I lost count of the time. He must have talked for an hour or more, and when it was quite over and he had confided everything, and the last drop of emotion had been drained from him he relaxed and managed to smile. I sensed his feeling of immense relief now that he had at last unburdened himself to a sympathetic ear. It was a pitiful story. Africa I knew, was full of human tragedy. Death is a frequent spectre, but memories are short and the ensuing trauma usually fades as swiftly as dew in the morning sun. In Lturungen's case the trauma had lasted almost his entire lifetime.

At the age of one he had walked into a fire. The family had been burning up goat dung. The outer layer of fire had cooled and looked as if it was no longer alight, yet underneath it was still white-hot. The pain was so intense it seems he couldn't cry out. He stood there paralysed, one foot in the fire, the other on the edge of it, his poor little brain numbed by the overwhelming agony. It was not until she became aware of the abhorrent smell of burning flesh that his mother was alerted to his plight.

By the time she had pulled him clear, part of the bone of his right foot and almost all his toes had been burned away. There were no tears, no emotion from Lturungen whatsoever. He was in severe shock. Fearing for his life, his parents decided he must be taken to hospital, a journey which involved many hours walking through the bush to a track, and then begging a lift in a passing lorry over miles of rough road.

The doctors treated him as best they could and sent him back home. Thereafter he had to be carried everywhere. His mother recalled that once the shock had worn off he cried continuously for almost a year.

Feet are as essential to a nomad as are hands to a pianist or eyes to a painter. Lturungen's inability to walk properly was for him an unmitigated disaster. It blighted his life. Life for the Samburu is in any case similar to walking a tightrope, dependent upon outwitting nature in all its vicissitudes on the one hand and predators, both human and animal, on the other.

The balance between survival and death is a fine one. As on the plains, the weakest animals are abandoned to become the prey of the lion and the leopard, so in the tribe there is no place for the disabled and infirm, and altruistically little sympathy for them either. A child born deformed is traditionally smothered at birth, but more unfortunate are those marred in childhood. They live a half life. Such children suffer both physical and mental anguish, for they are regarded as a burden to the tribe and are shown little love or consideration.

This is what befell Lturungen. He had to suffer both the pain of his foot and the desolation which arises from the withdrawal of affection. His mother, brothers and sister did no more than tolerate him. Only his father, then an old man, showed him any kindness and understanding.

When he was about seven Lturungen's uncle had the remarkable foresight to insist that he went back to hospital for a skin graft. The graft was to replace the flesh which had been burned away under the foot, and was to provide him with a pad on which to walk. Yet our soles and heels are formed of a type of skin which does not grow anywhere else on the body. The flesh taken from his thigh did indeed help him to walk a little, but being soft in texture could not withstand the wear and tear caused by walking, and always broke down and bled if he covered any distance. In hospital he was looked after by an Italian nurse who grew very fond of her plucky and very handsome young patient, and for the first time in his life Lturungen experienced the joy and comfort of motherly love.

After six months in hospital he returned home to find arrangements in hand for the circumcision of his next eldest brother. During the preparations for the ceremony the poor boy was drowned. It would have been unpropitious for the ceremony to be abandoned, and so like a lamb to the slaughter Lturungen was circumcised in place of his brother at the tender age of eight.

Even with the benefit of a skin graft, Lturungen could still not participate fully in tribal life, so his father intervened and in accord with government regulations but contrary to tribal laws, sent him as a boarder to the nearest primary school. This led to the loss of his identity as a Samburu by his mother and the rest of his family. They claimed it was not possible for him to hold a book in one hand and a spear in the other.

But at least Lturungen could learn to use his head, even if he couldn't use his feet. He did well enough at primary school to take the relatively unusual step for a Samburu of proceeding to secondary education. The school itself was in a much cooler climate than he was used to, and it suited his foot better. He was even able to engage in a little sport.

Now that he had finished school his worst fears were realised. Unable to get a job, he had no alternative but to go back to live with his family where the heat and the walking continued to break down the skin graft, leaving him immobile for days at a time and in grave danger of contracting an infection. Furthermore, although badly deformed, the bones which formed what was left of his foot continued to grow while the scar tissue around them did not. By now the bones were so bound by the surrounding skin that he had lost all movement in the foot, and consequently the muscles in his ankle and calf began to waste away through lack of exercise, restricting his mobility still further.

Because he had been away at school for so long, Lturungen had acquired no livestock of his own. He was destitute, and had to rely on his family for nourishment, or else buy maize with the little money Lpiritian gave him from time to time. Being circumcised early in life proved to be a major disadvantage for him. The circumcision age-set to which he belonged, the members of which were older than he, now became junior elders and were obliged to marry, and he with them.

Before he died his father had chosen wives for both Lpiritian and Buni, another brother, but in his wisdom he realised the break in tribal upbringing could make marriage within the tribe difficult if not impossible for his disabled son, so he decreed that Lturungen was free to marry any woman of his own choosing.

There was, however, one consequence of Lturungen's accident which his father had not foreseen. In the young boy's mind, the pain in his foot became associated not with its real cause but with the humping, lifting and carrying he experienced during his early days from an unsympathetic family and which, because of the tenderness of his wound, hurt him greatly. His mind associated the pain with this handling by others. As a consequence of this association, he could not now bear being touched on any part of his body.

I had observed how he had avoided all physical contact with those around him except for the formality of shaking hands and how, when my wife had kissed him, he had recoiled as if he had been stabbed. At the time I had put this reaction down to acute shyness; now I realised its true significance. How could he ever marry in such circumstances?

Samburu laws are strict and unyielding. Warriors and unmarried junior elders are not allowed to be seen eating by women and are prohibited from eating at all unless in the company of another. It meant that Lturungen often had to wait until it was dark before he took the first and only meal of the day, and would go without food altogether if he could not find a companion to join him. Neither was he allowed to build his own hut, and therefore had to beg accommodation at night from neighbours. Only if he lived away from the tribe in the nearest trading post could he escape these deprivations, but even this possibility was out of reach because he had no income and no prospect of a job.

When Lturungen's story was finished I wondered how fate could have been so cruel. Hemmed in on all sides by taboos, pain, disability, lack of opportunity and income, his life was one continuous struggle against great odds, with no let-up and no prospect of a solution save through the grace of God.

"There have been many times these last few months," he confided, "when I wished I was dead."

Yet I came to know his faith in a universal and merciful deity was such that he would never voluntarily end his life.

As the days went by, Lturungen gradually grew into his old self. His cheerfulness returned, he relaxed in the family atmosphere and savoured the delights and pleasures which Nairobi and its surrounds offered a stranger from up-country, but I became aware too that he was beginning to cling to us in the way a drowning man clings to a life raft, and this worried me. In us lay his only hope for the future, his only means of survival in a hostile world, his only way of escape from a life which held him captive.

We left Nairobi with heavy hearts. On the last evening before he returned to the north I stood with Lturungen on the edge of woodland overlooking the city. The sun had set in a sky ablaze with red and crimson and pink, half hidden by an armada of dark clouds riding the horizon. It is at this time of the evening in East Africa that the wind starts to blow in sudden fits as if to clear the air of the accumulated heat of the day before the long still night settles in. We stood a long time saying nothing, each absorbed in our own thoughts.

For me, the last light of day is always a time for contemplation and reflection. It is also a time when all the heartfelt thoughts, the deepest memories and impressions and the sadnesses of life come flocking back like sheep returning to the fold. On this particular evening I felt a sense of bewilderment, as if I had been presented with a task of great responsibility and knew not how to carry it out. It was as if I were in command of a rescue boat, had located the victim in the water and yet was unable to throw a lifeline to him because the tide of life was sweeping us inexorably apart.

The tropical darkness enfolded us. Lturungen's eyes were fixed on the skyline where the sun had set. He lingered, as if searching for the courage to ask the one final question which burned in his mind. Several times a word began to form on his lips, but no sound came forth.

"When shall I see you again?" he blurted out at last.

I had been expecting this question, and I didn't know how I should answer. I summoned up as much courage as I could, and explained that it might be several years before we returned to Kenya. We had two daughters at university and one was shortly to be married. As always, the constraint was money.

He stood silent, still looking into the distance and his eyes filled with tears. The life raft was slipping away from him. What momentarily had seemed a refuge and had buoyed up his spirits was now receding from his grasp, leaving him once more to flounder in the maelstrom of life.

CHAPTER THREE

England

warrior's necklace

AS THE WEEKS went by we felt remorse that we had left Lturungen bereft of a means of coming to terms with his circumstances, of giving him conviction in himself and in such abilities that he did have, even in giving him a ray of hope for the future.

We remembered how he grieved for his father, the one source of comfort and encouragement to him in childhood. He often referred to the way his father had calmed him when his foot was painful, and how he would stay awake and talk to him on those nights when he couldn't sleep. We were moved by the loneliness he so obviously felt as an outcast in a culture of which he was a part, but in which he could not participate. How sad it seemed that his life had been so blighted as the result of a single false step taken in childly innocence.

We agonised for weeks over the wisdom of bringing Lturungen to England. Africans, I had learned, were remarkably adaptable. Others had stayed with us before — even one from the Pokot tribe whose background was not dissimilar from Lturungen's. I had no doubt that he would adapt as easily as those before him, but my overriding concern was how we could prepare him for the eventual return to his tribal homeland after the comfort and security of an English home.

Then one day, a chance conversation with a friend led us to a foot specialist who expressed an interest in Lturungen's case. We were advised that nothing could be done to replace the underside of the foot. It would always give him some pain, especially when the skin broke down and became sore through walking. However, through surgery it might be possible to restore movement to the ankle and so strengthen his leg muscles and thus help him to walk with greater ease. The opportunity seemed too good to miss, and in the end we sent for him.

His joy in contemplating the journey knew no bounds, but it was soon tempered by practicalities. He required a passport. In order to obtain one, he needed both a birth certificate and an identity card. Before he could obtain a birth certificate he needed to know his date of birth. In common with most other Samburu, he had no idea when he was born.

He assumed he was about twenty. From his name — Lturungen — he decided he was born at the time of the rains, so he invented a birthday in June and assumed the age of twenty. Armed with the appropriate data he applied for his two documents, and then came up against what was for him a new and offensive facet of Kenyan life.

He travelled to the administrative centre of Maralal, completed the forms and paid the fee, but no identity card was forthcoming. Nor did it until he paid officialdom a handsome bribe. To one coming from a background where sharing is the norm and no request is refused without good reason, the concept of bribery was abhorrent. In his eyes, handing over the money was degrading not only for the official receiving it but also for him, for by participating in the practice he was condoning it. In tribal terms he had committed a crime and he felt sullied by it.

The episode played on his conscience long afterwards. "I waited four days in that place for that card," he related to me later. "Each day I was told it would be ready next day. It cost me nearly all my savings in lodgings. I couldn't understand what was going on, and then someone took me aside and told me I would never get it unless I paid over some more money. I tell you, Roger, I would never have done it if it had been for anything less than coming to England."

Worse was to come. Our friends in Nairobi played a vital part in acquiring the passport and delivering him to the airport, but once he was out of their care and through the customs and into the departure area, tribal rivalry loomed in the guise of officialdom. An opportunity to travel to England is sought after by many Kenyans, and achieved by few.

What business had this shabbily dressed individual to be travelling to the West? Why hadn't the chance come to those in authority, those wielding power over the hapless traveller, the gatekeepers of the national airport, and why should this Samburu, this nomad of all people, be granted such a privilege?

His passport was taken away to be checked. It was not returned. When the time came for departure he was refused a boarding card because he had no passport. He returned to the immigration officials who demanded to see his identity card, but that had been left in Nairobi for safekeeping. "Very well then, no identity card, no passport."

Lturungen protested. He could not have obtained his passport in the first place without an identity card — surely that was proof enough he had one? There was an argument. He was accused of being a Somali posing as a Kenyan. It cut him to the quick. It was the equivalent of calling him a bastard. The Samburu hated the Somali with good reason, and the officials knew it. Somali guerrillas had crossed the border and massacred Samburu in large numbers. One of Lturungen's brothers had been among the many killed.

In desperation Lturungen traipsed back and forth between the two authorities, the one the government, the other the airline, trapped in a game of cat-and-mouse.

Two minutes before the flight was due to depart he was ordered on board, but without a passport. It was intimidation at its worst. Ten hours of flight, only to be turned back at his destination was uppermost in his mind.

He turned to the passenger on his left. "Have you got your passport?" he asked.

"Of course".

He turned to the passenger on his right and got the same response.

They were businessmen. They had the knowledge and experience of foreign travel. Both confirmed that without a passport you would not gain entry to Britain. He would be returned home on the next flight.

Lturungen could neither eat nor sleep. He sat rooted to his chair, engulfed in the deepest depression. He felt small and insignificant; helpless in the hands of authority. It was a nightmare to be on board that huge machine, flying at an unimaginable height and speed towards an inhospitable land.

He was in the company of people who were in a class quite beyond him. He observed their suits, their patent leather shoes, their dresses and jewellery, and compared them with his own worn clothes and the plimsolls on his feet. These were people of substance. He recalled their suitcases and smart travelling gear, and he thought of his own small bag and his two brown paper parcels. He looked round the cabin and felt hopelessly alone. Everyone else seemed to be so relaxed, their affairs in order, their destinations secure.

A journey to England had been beyond his wildest dreams. Now he began to doubt the wisdom of reaching for something ostensibly beyond his grasp.

At Heathrow the other passengers disembarked. Lturungen remained in his seat; he could not face another confrontation with the authorities, and he wanted to put off as long as possible the shame of being returned to Kenya, the ridicule he would receive at home and the despair he would feel at letting us down after all the arrangements we had made on his behalf. Then the stewardess approached him and told him he must leave the aircraft immediately.

She had his passport in her hand!

Lturungen recovered from his ordeal remarkably quickly. Although Heathrow, with its bustle of people and traffic, and the grey and damp September day must have seemed strange to him, he made light of it and generously asserted he felt confident and relaxed in my company.

Before we set out in the car and drove down to the West Country, we each had a cup of tea and a Danish pastry. Cake was a new experience for Lturungen, and he eyed the delicacy apprehensively. With a little persuasion he took a small bite. As his teeth sank into the sweet and succulent texture, his face lit up in a broad grin. Never had he experienced such sweetness before; this must be the food of gods. He took a sensuous delight in every bite. If this was a foretaste of England, then he was definitely going to enjoy himself here!

We were right about African adaptability. Lturungen installed himself in our home as a family cat settles itself into a favourite chair. His feline ability to withstand the toughest conditions and yet take a greedy delight in unaccustomed luxury seemed to be a Samburu characteristic.

He had never experienced a bed as soft and as comfortable as the one he now occupied. He piled on all the bedclothes, slid out of sight under them and spent the night comatose. At home he would invariably be up with the dawn, but here we were shaking him awake at gone 9.00 in the morning. At other times he would flop into an arm-chair, bury himself in cushions and drape his legs over the arms, smiling with confident pleasure as he did so. And when he was cold he would take a mat and curl up like a cat on the floor in front of the stove, oblivious of everyone and everything around him.

He possessed a gravitational pull which made everything in the home revolve around him. He influenced our domestic arrangements, our weekends away, and even our behaviour in his company. He would ask for cake, or bread, or tea, and somehow we found ourselves scampering around to his every beck and call.

"I feel perfectly at ease in this place," he would say cheerfully and with an air of permanency which took me by surprise.

Quick to learn, he reinforced his occupancy by taking charge of things around the house. The motor mower was a great source of pleasure, and he became expert at cutting the grass. He commandeered the kitchen sink and excelled at washing and wiping up, and he took upon himself the responsibility of opening the door to visitors and answering the telephone, although it was some weeks before we could rely on him to hold the handset the right way up.

Sometimes things caught him unawares. When the temperature began to fall I switched on the central heating. He leaned casually against a radiator one day, and let out a howl of amazement when he burned himself. Then there followed a lengthy discussion about how we heated our homes, and he took himself on a safari around the house, following the hot water pipes from room to room.

On another occasion he walked unsuspectingly through a clump of stinging nettles. Believing he had been bitten, he broke into a run to get away from what he thought was the offending animal.

The fax, the telephone and the computer terminal in the office intrigued him, but he was most captivated by the roller blinds, pulling them down and then giving the cord a little tug to send them reeling up to the window top time and time again. The simplicity of this small item pleased him more than all the electronic gadgetry he came across.

"My goodness," he said after about the fiftieth time he had released the blinds, "you people really are clever to think of something like this!"

I took a photograph of him sitting at my office desk, talking nonchalantly into the telephone and dressed in newly acquired clothes. It was to impress his friends from the Westernised tribes he met from time to time in the nearest trading post to his home.

Of all his clothes, the most prized possession was the yellow tie I had given him. I had no idea of the status a tie conferred on a Kenyan. We had a rather special engagement to attend which called for a tie. It had not occurred to me that he had never worn one, even at school, and still less that he had always aspired to own one. The glee on his face was something to behold when I handed it over.

"In Kenya only bosses wear ties," he said incredulously, and then with childish pretence, "now I'm a boss". Then consternation because he didn't know how it should be tied. I showed him; he practised assiduously in front of the mirror again and again until he could do it perfectly, preening and titivating as he did so with all the vanity of a warrior.

I learned afterwards that ownership of a tie meant much more to him than that. It was as if he had been awarded a high honour; in his mind's eye a tie was linked irrevocably with the British way of life. Ownership of one was akin to bestowing him with British nationality. It overcame all the differences of colour, religion, upbringing and education. It made him one of us.

Perhaps the most endearing thing about Lturungen was his grin. It won him friends wherever he went. He had a mouth which naturally turned up at the corners, even when he was morose, but when he grinned he seemed to grin from ear to ear while his eyes danced with merriment.

Other Africans who had stayed with us were younger and occupied their time by attending school. We wanted Lturungen to get used to life in England before having the operation on his foot and being bedridden for some considerable time. We needed some means of keeping him busy, and before he arrived I hit upon the idea of sending him to school, not to learn but to teach.

I contacted a number of head teachers. "How about a tribal warrior in full dress coming to talk to the children?" I enquired.

Most welcomed the opportunity, and I drew up a tentative programme.

"Bring some warrior's clothes and a spear and toothbrush sticks and red ochre," I had written to Lturungen. He was a personable young man, but there was a niggle at the back of my mind regarding his ability as a communicator. I needn't have worried. There was his smile and his knowledge of English, but more than that he had an additional asset which we had not counted upon, and that was charisma.

We sat down and worked out what he might say about his family and his tribe and their lifestyle. Lturungen was not short of ideas. We rehearsed for several evenings, and I realised he knew a thing or two about showmanship as well.

He had managed to bring with him all the gear I had requested. Now that he was officially a junior elder Lturungen thankfully no longer wore the long hair of a warrior. Had he done so, most of the things in the house would have been spattered with red ochre. Instead he had acquired a red ochre-coated wig, carefully wrapped in layers of newspaper to protect the rest of his belongings.

There was a red and white *nanga*, a variety of beads and bangles and bracelets, some his own and some borrowed from his brothers, and a six-foot spear which, before setting out on his journey, he had disassembled and wrapped in brown paper so that it was not obviously a weapon. His toothbrush sticks were placed in the refrigerator to keep them fresh and green, and the powdered red ochre was mixed with lard so that it could be applied to his body.

The day of Lturungen's first assignment dawned. I had badly miscalculated the time he would take to adorn himself in his finery. All four of our daughters had been in and out of the bathroom, eaten breakfast, and left the house before he emerged triumphantly in all his glory — a striking figure to behold.

The wig entirely covered his hair and looked authentic; hundreds of delicate braids hanging down to the small of his back. Lturungen had always seemed a strongly masculine figure, and I was taken aback to find that he now adopted the mannerisms of a girl. He rearranged the braids when they fell forward of his shoulders either by a quick toss of the chin to flick them over his back, or by taking both hands and gathering them up behind his nape.

His chest, neck and cheeks were covered in a gleaming layer of red ochre; a variety of ornaments decorated his forehead, and beads hung in chains on his naked limbs and torso. Tall, slim and elegant, his supple body was the envy of many. A *nanga* covered him only from the waist to the knees. Fearing he would be cold in the autumn air and concerned about the effect of red ochre on the car upholstery, we decided to dedicate an old quilted anorak to the cause.

I remember that first morning well. The venue was a small rural primary school. Lturungen's entry was dramatic. As he strode through the playground, spear in hand, beads and bangles jingling and the greasy warpaint shining in the sun, the children stopped their play and subsided into stunned silence. One of the mothers standing just in front of me caught her neighbour by the arm.

"Gawd!" she exclaimed, "he'll terrify the pants off my kids!"

There was consternation in the staff room when Lturungen loomed at the doorway. They had expected something out of the ordinary, but this display of raw warriorhood, armed, and at such close quarters, caught them off guard. When he regained his composure, the head teacher sat the children in neat rows down the length of the hall.

All eyes were glued on Lturungen. There were a few introductory remarks and then the floor was his.

With a fine sense of the dramatic, he drew himself up to his full height, spear in hand, and eyed the children. For a moment he said nothing. The atmosphere was electric. Then he spoke in his native language.

"*Eserian ngera.*" Pause.

The tension increased.

"You didn't understand me, did you?" he said in English.

No response from the children.

"I'll try again. *Jambo watoto*," he said, this time in Swahili.

Silence.

"You didn't understand me that time either, did you?"

Suddenly the children came alive; they had tumbled to it! He was playing some kind of game.

"No we didn't," the braver ones volunteered a little self-consciously.

"All right, I'll try once more. Good morning children," he said in perfect English.

The tension turned to relief. The hall was full of smiling faces. He had won his audience over in seven short sentences.

"Good morning, Sir," they chorused in reply, and Lturungen's face was lit up in a disarming grin.

The children loved him. They drank in his description of the tribe, the wild animals and the living conditions. So that his audience should not get bored, he wove into his talk a number of high points. He was good at the technique of question and answer, sometimes answering the questions himself, sometimes leaving it to the audience.

"Now what food do you think we eat? Cake? No. Bread? No. Vegetables? No."

And then heavily, "Our main food is blood and milk. I repeat, blood and milk."

The young audience was understandably appalled at this revelation, and adopted the appropriate vocal and facial expressions. I noticed, however, that the effect on the lady teachers was greater. They had been wooed by his seductive smile, his slim body and graceful limbs, his muscular torso and his dreamy eyes, and had gazed on him in admiration. Now he was feigning Dracula instead of Cupid, and they were not quite sure how to handle it.

Lturungen worked his audience well. At one stage when the children were hanging on his every word he said, "If I were to ask two of you to go and stand one behind the other over there in the far corner of the hall ..."

A forest of hands went up, begging to be chosen.

He ploughed on as if nothing had happened. "... and I was to take up my spear and throw it as hard as I could ..."

Hands were raised still higher.

"... it would go right through the two of you". All hands came down immediately.

"That is how sharp this spear is," Lturungen continued impressively while the children looked with considerable apprehension at the weapon he was holding.

The toothbrush demonstration was a great success.

"You see," said Lturungen, "we don't have toilets. For toilets we use a convenient bush, and we use leaves for toilet paper, and for toothbrushes we use sticks."

Then he chose a stick from the bundle he had with him and began peeling the outer skin from one end. He put the peeled end between his molars and chewed vigorously, walking around the hall staring up at the ceiling. With his head on one side, he made exploring noises with his tongue and considering noises just like Tigger when he was tasting honey.

A small gasp from the children when he extracted the stick and revealed a nicely formed brush head.

Holding the stick like a toothbrush Lturungen proceeded to clean his teeth. There was rapt attention in the hall, some of the children making teeth-cleaning shapes with their mouths as they were carried away by their imagination.

"And very important too. Don't forget to clean the inside of your teeth as well, and you will be like me and never need to visit a dentist." He opened his mouth wide to prove the point, revealing teeth that would be the envy of a film star.

Belief in a universal God is an important aspect of Samburu life, and Lturungen was determined to cover this too.

"We have no churches and no Sundays in our tribe," he recounted. "You see, we believe it is necessary to pray to God at all times and in all places. When I was young my mother taught me to pray when I go to bed, before I get up in the morning, and each time I wake up during the night. I advise you to do the same and to thank God for all the good things he has given us on this earth."

There was no doubting Lturungen's sincerity, and the children were impressed.

He still had one trick up his sleeve and that was the red ochre, or the warpaint as he called it. He had brought along a small tub of the stuff and we had given him some cotton buds to apply it. The youngsters queued for ages to have their faces painted. The ochre was applied sparingly to cheeks, noses and foreheads, and each was warned not to get it on their clothes.

What a transformation when Lturungen strode out of the school! The children no longer stood hushed in the playground. He was the Pied Piper and they streamed after him, those nearest

Lturungen at an English primary school

touching his *nanga*, his beads, his hair. As he disappeared out of the gate with a flourish, faces were pressed against the railings, determined to catch the last glimpse of their warrior hero.

Lturungen had prepared two talks, the shorter one for primary schools and a second, including circumcision and marriage, which stimulated great interest among pupils of the local comprehensive schools. As time went by and his fame spread, he found himself preparing versions for infants and for a variety of adult audiences as well.

On one occasion he was asked to speak to a junior assembly at a large comprehensive school. He spoke for an hour and quarter to an audience of five hundred, and you could have heard a pin drop, so well did he hold their attention. When it was over we began to pack up and put his things in the car. During the short time it took for the senior assembly to file into the hall, word of his talk had spread and the senior pupils demanded to be treated no less favourably, so a reluctant head teacher abandoned the programme he had planned and Lturungen found himself addressing a second audience of similar size that same morning.

He was not greeted with the same degree of enthusiasm at all schools. At one comprehensive, the teacher introduced him to a very bored-looking assembly at the beginning of the school day. From their appearance you might have thought that every one of those children was suffering from a hangover. The headmaster's attempts to arouse an interest were of no avail.

Lturungen was introduced. He stepped up to the front of the stage.

"Good morning everybody," he said in a loud clear voice.

The school stared sullenly back at him.

Silence in response to a greeting is insulting behaviour, especially to an African, and Lturungen was not going to put up with this impudence. Spear in hand, he leapt to the floor and challenged them.

"What's the matter with you all this morning? Are you still in your beds?" And then slowly and deliberately, "I will say it again — good morning everybody."

The stratagem worked, whether through shock or intrigue I do not know, but the school returned a rousing "Good morning", and Lturungen had achieved the attention he desired.

Lturungen was a born catechist. I realised he had the makings of an excellent teacher.

"Now Roger," he would say, "what do you remember of this or that tribal custom?"

Like a small boy at school I would rack my brain and try to recall what it was he had taught me earlier. I was never quite sure why I so readily succumbed to such impertinence from one less than half my age. Primary school children in particular enjoyed this kind of teaching which he combined with some blackboard work. At one school the pupils were keen to learn to count in the Maa language. Lturungen wrote the numbers on the board and drilled the youngsters in pronunciation, first by getting the whole class to follow him and then picking out individuals and pointing to specific numbers. This was followed by the theory of firelighting using two sticks, a bit about how the women and children spent their time in the *nkang*, and then how you set about skinning an animal.

After what was an imaginative excursion into nomadic living he returned to the cerebral discipline of learning and remembering. "Now how many of you can still count from one to ten?"

One hand shot up. Several children sniggered when they saw whose hand it was.

"What's your name?"

"Peter."

"Right Peter, start counting."

"*Nabo, Aare, Uuni, Oongwan, Imet, Ile, Sapa, Iseat, Saal, Tomon,*" the youngster said obediently.

A gasp went up from around the room. The only child who could remember all the numbers correctly was the boy regarded as being the dullest in the class.

Understandably it was hard work handling an audience of mixed ages and interests, but Lturungen proved he could manage this as well. On one occasion he gave a talk in a town with a large retirement population. He kept everybody happy by addressing remarks to each age group in turn, speaking loudly and clearly to the elderly, handing out toothbrush sticks to the children, discussing Samburu clothing and ornaments with the ladies and fielding questions from a number of old colonial buffers in the back rows.

One of them made himself quite objectionable by trying to monopolise Lturungen's attention, and at the same time flaunting a limited knowledge of Swahili. There came a time when Lturungen felt he had had enough of this treatment. He turned to the offender and said "I see you know Swahili. Let me do a little test for you."

To the amusement of the audience he began to quiz the man on a number of basic words. He got very quickly out of his depth and lapsed into silence, whereupon Lturungen continued his talk uninterrupted.

The Samburu are renowned for their courage and discipline, and the British were not slow to recognise their skill as soldiers during the long years when the then Northern Frontier District was under military control. The inhospitable climate in this part of Africa is a challenge to survival and one to which the Samburu and their neighbouring tribes have adapted particularly well. However the constant struggle against drought, disease, marauding animals and warring neighbours, together with the ever-present spectre of death, serves to steel the nerve and strengthen the resolve. Stoicism and valour are inbred, as is the sense of plucky self-confidence.

These characteristics were discernible in Lturungen. When we first met him in Nairobi I was surprised that his few belongings were packed into a smart rucksack instead of being wrapped up in a paper parcel as I had expected. When I asked him how he had obtained the rucksack he answered modestly that he had been given it for saving some New Zealand tourists from the Shifta.

One afternoon in the school holidays when he was tending the family's goats, he had been approached by three white tourists who were hiking through the bush. They were making for one of the tourist lodges but had lost their way. Lturungen called to his younger brother to look after the animals so that he could accompany the strangers to their destination. At that time the Shifta were prevalent in the area, and they hadn't gone far before they were surrounded by armed bandits demanding their money, clothes and belongings.

It was a life-threatening situation. The Shifta invariably shot their victims. Lturungen, however, stood his ground and showing no emotion, offered them his own life on condition that the others were spared. He argued that the tourists had entrusted themselves to his care, and that it was he who had unwittingly led them into this situation. It seems that his sincerity and his charisma prevailed, for the Shifta let them all go after relieving them of what money they had. The rucksack, together with a few items of clothing, had been his reward from the very shaken but extremely grateful travellers.

There were, however, two occasions during his stay with us when Lturungen did express anxiety, and once when he completely broke down. We were glad that he felt safe and secure enough with us to give vent to his emotions in our company, for back in his tribe the display of such emotion would not have been acceptable.

The operation on his foot worried him greatly. It had been established that some major surgery would be required. He would have been less concerned if it was to be carried out under a general anaesthetic, but the limitations of the specialist's private surgery meant that only a local anaesthetic could be used.

From the time he could remember he had lived with pain. Pain had moulded his attitude to life. Pain had eaten into his sensibility. It had constrained his activities. It had conspired to force him into a sedentary life, so unnatural to one born and bred out of doors. His life was hemmed in by pain, the silent enemy within, an affliction which he could share with no one else and which because of its invisibility enlisted no support and no sympathy from without.

He told me how Karaito, a wild and impulsive child, had once stamped on his foot in a fit of temper and how he, Lturungen, had thumped him so hard in the chest out of frustration that the boy had coughed up blood. Lturungen, who had exercised so much self-will to hide his suffering from his family, was filled with remorse at the memory of his own petulance when he related the story. His usual cheerful disposition had concealed even from us the degree of pain he suffered, and it was only now that we recognised the extent of his misery. Every endeavour in life had first to be weighed against the discomfort it would generate. Even though he knew he would feel no real sensation, the thought of being conscious while part of the bone was amputated — a formidable undertaking for anyone — made the operation for him particularly daunting. Then again, because he had become so inured to pain he could not conceive of a time when he might be free of it. Had he been able to do so, that in itself might have made the ordeal seem more bearable.

Lturungen needed a massive amount of support and encouragement from us in the days leading up to the operation, and were it not for our mutual trust and confidence I doubt whether he would have gone through with it.

The other occasion when he lost his composure was most unexpected and took me by surprise. We were driving up the M5 past Bristol when he suddenly grabbed my arm. I swerved.

"You don't have elephants in these parts do you?" he exclaimed in alarm. He had seen the elephant on the road sign for Bristol Zoo, and it had made him greatly agitated.

I was not pleased that he had interfered with the steering and told him so. Then I went on to explain that there was one elephant in the area, but that she was in a zoo. He was still ill-at-ease.

"What's a zoo?"

There were two game parks not so far from his home in Kenya, so I did my best to explain. "You know how tourists on safari watch the game walk around them from the safety of those big lorries? Well, a zoo is the other way round. The animals are behind bars and the people walk around outside and view them."

Lturungen was very unhappy with this idea even though I assured him it was all very safe for humans. At first I assumed he had confused the sign for a zoo with the ones I had shown him earlier warning of deer on the roads. No wonder he was alarmed, if in his mind's eye he was imagining the carnage which would ensue if a herd of elephants formed up at the edge of the hard shoulder and then ambled across the motorway.

Then it dawned on me what was troubling him. I had always supposed the Samburu's arch enemy to be the lion, and so did the children at the schools he visited, but we were wrong; it was the elephant.

"The elephant is the animal we fear most," he would say. "You see, an African elephant is more than twice as tall as me, and it can weigh up to eight tons. Now the problem is that the prickly thorn hedges that we put round our villages to stop the lions do not stop the elephants, so it can be very dangerous if an elephant comes crashing through my bedroom in the middle of the night when I am asleep.

"They will squash you flat! You can feel the earth tremble when an elephant comes near, so that is why we sleep on the ground and not on beds like the Maasai. When we feel the earth tremble we wake up immediately and grasp our spears."

To see the devastation an elephant causes uprooting trees is a fearsome sight, and the damage they can inflict on a wooded area in a very short time is horrifying. Like most of the wild animals, they are unlikely to be dangerous if you keep your distance from them but they are so unpredictable that you would be foolhardy to approach close to one.

Lturungen recalled how, as a boy, he had been with a group of neighbours on the way to a celebration. Their journey led through some woodland. They were all of them in high spirits. Way ahead of the group was a woman who was always the life and soul of a party; she was busily chattering to the others and did not realise she had disturbed a large bull elephant which had been obscured from sight by the trees. The animal was maddened by this intrusion and as she came close the elephant charged and, plucking her up in his trunk, flung her high into the air. Her body smashed against a tree and her remains fell in a heap to the ground. The sudden and unprovoked savagery of this attack remained with him as an indelible memory.

Wendy is the only elephant at Bristol Zoo. I hastened to reassure Lturungen that she was an Indian elephant and that Indian elephants were tame. They were used as working animals, and people could also ride on them. Lturungen simply refused to believe this and maintained that all elephants, whatever their origin, were extremely dangerous. Nevertheless my remarks aroused his curiosity, and when he was recovering from his operation he returned to the subject on several occasions. Gradually his curiosity got the better of him. Despite his fear of elephants he wanted to see the supposedly tame one. He didn't believe such a thing existed, but he had to be sure. After all, we had shown him many things during his stay which he could never have imagined and, well, there just might be some truth in it. The thought of going back home and being able to say he had touched a live elephant appealed to him, and yet he realised no one would believe him — unless of course I took a photograph. Yes, that was it. I had to take a photograph as proof of his exploit.

We realised he would not settle until we had taken him to Bristol. I rang the zoo and explained our mission. They were sympathetic. Wendy's keeper was on holiday, but his assistant would be on hand and we were to ask for him on arrival.

It was a cold, overcast and windless November day. Lturungen sat in a thick overcoat in his wheelchair, and wore gloves and a scarf to keep out the chill. Wendy was in her quarters when we arrived. The assistant keeper led us through the perimeter fence to a side gate so that we could get close to the animal when she emerged. Then he laid a trail of food out into the pen and across to where we were positioned.

Presently Wendy came out, sniffed the air, urinated and then followed the trail. My wife was standing with the wheelchair close up by the gate. I was some little distance away, camera in hand. Wendy was in no hurry. She picked up the food slowly and daintily without bothering about us. Bit by bit she got nearer the gate.

I could see Lturungen beginning to sit well back in his seat. Then she reached the gate and put her trunk over to pick up the few last pieces of food on our side. Lturungen was somewhat shocked; he said nothing, but pressed himself deep into the chair and raised his feet off the footrest in alarm. When she had consumed everything, Wendy lifted her head and looked at Lturungen. Their eyes met. She lifted her trunk and blew into his face.

Lturungen let out a strangled cry and held up his hands. The next moment her trunk was exploring his lap very gently. Summoning all his courage he put out his hand and stroked her. I took the photograph.

In a way it was like a reunion; he was beaming from ear to ear, and she was delighted to have some respite from boredom. Despite the November gloom Lturungen's eyes were filled with sunlight. This was a Red Letter Day for him. Although he had seen and done so many wonderful things during his time in England, he never ever imagined he would make friends with an elephant. It remained the subject of conversation for long afterwards.

One day a letter arrived postmarked Isiolo. Although Isiolo is a town many miles south of the area in which Lturungen lived, it is nevertheless the furthest the postal service reaches. We had dropped in at home between two of Lturungen's speaking engagements. The afternoon was an important one for him; it was the first time he was speaking to a mixed audience in a public building. The occasion had attracted the attention of the media and I was anxious it should go well. I looked at the letter as it lay on the dining room table, and for some inexplicable reason it filled me with foreboding.

I wasn't sure what to do — should I hand over the letter or keep it from him until after he had fulfilled his engagement? Our relationship had always been open and honest. It was the only letter he had received while staying with us, and it seemed wrong to conceal it from him. I knew in any case that he believed in facing fairly and squarely anything that life threw at him. I gave him the letter as we were driving along, fervently hoping it would not wreck his performance. He opened it and read it. He said nothing, folded it up and put it away. I knew intuitively though that it had caused him great anguish.

The talk went splendidly. Lturungen was on top form and so many people wanted to speak to him afterwards that we had some difficulty in getting away. He was silent all the way back and disappeared into his bedroom as soon as we got home. I found him there an hour or so later, weeping effusively. Life had been kinder to him during the last few months before he left Kenya. Three older friends of his were working in Archer's Post, a little trading post not so very far from where his family were living, and they earned enough money between them to rent a small room. Knowing of his predicament Lturungen had been invited to share it with them free of charge. It had made all the difference to his life; not only did he have constant companionship, but living there freed him from tribal laws and restrictions. He had a roof over his head and he could eat as and when he wanted to.

The letter was from John, the closest of his companions, and it was to say that all three of them had just been awarded places at a Teacher's Training college and would be gone by the time he got back from England.

Coming from such a different background and culture it was difficult for me to imagine the deprivation that Lturungen suffered in the *nkang*, but from the way he wept I could see that for him it was as if his world had come to an end. Earlier he had confessed about weeping when he felt life was becoming too difficult for him, and on these occasions he had to hide away where no friend or family could see him.

He wept all night, and we felt utterly helpless. We knew of no solution to his problems. Because even in the depth of despair he still could not bear to have an arm put around him, we were unable to give him any physical comfort. By morning the crying had stopped, but he was totally exhausted. Kind words and sympathy gradually dispelled the dark clouds of despondency. By now we felt as emotionally drained as he did, and I longed to be able to arrange for some semblance of an ordinary life for him.

CHAPTER FOUR

London

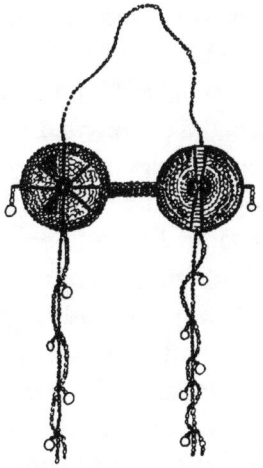

woman's rain-making necklace

LTURUNGEN WAS gripping my hand tightly like a small child. He was bemused and bewildered and not a little scared.

"How do you find your way around here?" he asked, with a mixture of admiration and anxiety. "If you weren't with me I wouldn't know where to go or what to do. I would be completely lost as if I was in a wilderness."

His usually placid face was puckered with concern. I remember I laughed; it was a foolish thing to do. His innate Samburu self-confidence, which normally carried him effortlessly over life's vicissitudes had been breached, and I had taken a perverse delight in it. I felt shame course through my veins as I remembered that this situation was as frightening to him as being in the bush would be for me, with only a spear for protection from marauding animals.

The cause of Lturungen's anxiety was not the fear of wild

animals, nor the Somali Shifta which had ravaged and plundered so much of his homeland in the years since British rule. No — it was instead the shock and exhilaration of London.

We were walking down the Haymarket towards Trafalgar Square. The roar of busy London streets was for him far more alarming than the roar of a lion, the incessant onslaught of vehicles worse than any stampede of buffalo. The cacophony disturbed his poise. He was engulfed in a melée of turning wheels, stifling fumes and a tide of people pressing in on him on all sides. His limbs were jarred by the hardness of London streets, and his feet ached from unyielding pavements.

Then suddenly out in Trafalgar Square he saw there was life other than the press of human bodies. There were birds — birds more numerous than he had ever seen before, and so tame! He ran towards them; he crouched down, and to his surprise they didn't fly away. Instead they came towards him, hundreds of grey bodies and jerking heads in search of food. Such tameness was unknown to him. One actually perched on his hand, and then another and another, and on his arms and then his shoulders one by one they came. Then he stood up, pigeons flying about his head and perched along the length of his outstretched arms, the antithesis of a scarecrow. For a moment he was entranced. London no longer held any fear for him. The sights, the sounds and the crowds ceased to register in his consciousness. He was in his own world of fluttering wings and cooing bills.

Then I shattered the spell. "Lturungen!" I shouted, "watch out for your clothes, you'll get pigeon muck all over them."

My voice cut through his reverie. The dreamy look fell from his face; he stared at his arms and shook them violently, releasing an explosion of flapping wings and falling feathers. He returned to me shamefacedly but still clean. His clothes were his pride and joy — his two pairs of new trousers, two shirts, his smart green zip-up jersey, his anorak, socks and three pairs of blue underpants. He would have worn them all at once if he had been given the chance. The limp, faded, well-worn and well-washed secondhand garments he had arrived in from Kenya had been put aside and for the first time in his life he wore clothes that were new.

From Trafalgar Square we made our way up St Martin's Lane towards Neal Street and The Bead Shop. Beads and clothes were the only things Lturungen had expressed an interest in acquiring. As we wove our way through the crowds I hoped he would not be disappointed. Earlier that morning I had taken him to Harrods. His experience of shopping had until then embraced only the essentials of life: cloth for *nangas*, tea, sodas, sandals and basic foodstuffs to supplement the drought-limited supply of milk and blood. There was neither the money nor the opportunity to purchase more. I thought Harrods would be an Aladdin's Cave for him; I thought his eyes would feast on the twinkling, sparkling array of jewellery, necklaces and baubles, and I imagined the appeal they would have for one whose youth had been spent bedecked with a gaudy array of beads and trinkets. After the pungent smells of dung and leather and wood smoke I could envisage his senses being transported by the sweet and seductive scent of the perfumery, and I thought he would be enthralled by the range and variety of provisions in the Food Hall.

But I was mistaken. Coming from a culture where nothing is personally owned except livestock, wives and weapons, and where barter is the order of the day — ten cows for a wife, a goat for a spear — the European's preoccupation with material goods and monetary values was entirely alien to him. He had the greatest difficulty in relating the value of money to merchandise, nor was he easily seduced by the eye. The beauty or attractiveness of an object held no interest for him if it was of no practical use. In my enthusiasm we had walked the length and breadth of the store, but the only thing which caught his attention was the meat hanging in the butcher's. He cast an alert but dismissive eye over all else. A store which purported to sell everything held nothing for him.

Our expedition to The Bead Shop was more successful. His

approach could be described as decisive. Around us a number of female shoppers, who seemed to have no set purpose in mind, flitted from tray to tray like butterflies alighting on a bead here, a metal trinket there as they took their fancy. Lturungen sized up the array of goods on display like an expert and settled down to select from the few trays which held beads of the shape and colour which interested him. As to be expected, he chose only those which reflected the traditional colours used by the Samburu. Size was critical; all the beads had to be small, the exception being the rather larger green ones traditionally worn by young children. Beads had to be round not oval, and translucent beads were unacceptable. However, after some persuasion I did eventually get him to choose a few especially decorative items for his mother. It was a serious business. It was, after all, an exercise in Samburu haute couture. Accordingly, Lturungen not unreasonably adopted the same air of gravity and attentiveness as one would expect of a lady choosing a hat for Royal Ascot.

The rest of the time was filled with activity as we attempted to pack in as much sightseeing as possible — the Tower, Westminster Abbey, Buckingham Palace and St Paul's Cathedral. At one stage we caught sight of a posse of Lifeguards. Lturungen couldn't believe his eyes! To him they were the most incongruous sight imaginable. Firstly he was unfamiliar with horses as there were none in the part of the world he came from; secondly everybody with anything to do with animals walked with them. No tribesman with any dignity would contemplate riding on an animal, and he wondered why we should debase ourselves in this way; thirdly it was incomprehensible to him that in the rush of London traffic the British, of all people, should choose to use such an ungainly and slow means of transport. His eye took in the helmets and the plumes. The gold and red of the uniforms shone; they looked a magnificent sight as they picked their way down Constitution Hill. "Who are these people?" he asked, his voice a mixture of awe and disbelief.

"Oh those," I answered casually, "those are our warriors."

Inwardly I was bursting with laughter. I could imagine what was going on in his head. Proud warrior though he had been, red ochre had nothing on the resplendent red of these uniforms, and no amount of beads could equal the splendour of the golden breastplates. Even the plumes of the helmets were more striking than a warrior's headpiece. Thereafter his admiration for the British grew appreciably.

Lturungen did not see his first boat until we came to London. He was fascinated by the Thames, its width, the size of the bridges, the fact that the river seemed to flood twice a day, even though there was no rain, and that the water was grey rather than brown. If I hadn't hauled him back he would have run down the embankment steps to taste it.

His sense of wonder at seeing the Thames was surpassed only when we took him to the coast. We stood on the cliffs above Sidmouth on a lovely autumn day.

"My! this one is big," he kept murmuring to himself as the sea stretched away to the horizon. Down on the beach he scooped up water in his hands, then spat it out in disgust. "But it's salt!" he exclaimed in astonishment. "All that water and you can't drink it! What a waste! What a terrible waste!"

It was a cold iron-grey afternoon in London, but I could see a river trip would give Lturungen a great deal of pleasure. I still had one surprise for him, and that was the Greenwich foot tunnel. We took the train to Island Gardens and walked through the park to the river's edge. We looked across to Greenwich and I told him it was from there we would take a boat. Lturungen could not imagine how we could cross such a wide stretch of water dry foot. When we walked through the tunnel he was incredulous.

"Fancy walking underneath a river," he kept saying. "They will never believe me when I get home — not even the educated ones!"

There was rain in the wind when we boarded.

The concept of a boat was novel to him. His excitement was

immense. He insisted on sitting in the open, right up in the bow. Although we brushed the moisture off the seats he never found the time to sit down. Instead he jigged around like a six-year old.

"Roger," he said, "what holds the boat up?" I tried to explain about buoyancy and that air was lighter than water, but he didn't stop to listen. When we were under way he was peering over the bow in astonishment as the Thames slipped past the hull. The questions came thick and fast.

"Roger, where does all the water go?"

"It doesn't go anywhere, the boat just moves through it."

"Then what makes the boat move — is it the wind, and how do you make it go where you want it to?"

Again I did my best to describe the action of a propeller in water and the property of a rudder, but he was off again, this time going aft to see what was happening at the stern. Then he was back, leaning first over one side and then the other watching the water, the banks and the buildings go past.

He reminded me of those dogs you sometimes see in the back of farmers' vans, so interested in seeing what is going on and wanting to see out of both sides at once, and racing to and fro in an attempt to do so.

I was perished, and would have gladly gone into the cabin to get out of the wind, but as Lturungen was determined to remain outside I felt obliged to stay with him. When at last Tower Bridge came into view he requested I took a photograph of him in the foreground. I wondered what they would make of the picture back home. The all-pervading greyness would make it look as if it were in monochrome. A river they knew to be brown was grey; the sky they knew to be blue was also grey, and unless they had been to Archer's Post, the crossing point on the Wuaso Ngiro, his family would never have understood the significance of a bridge.

The moment I had taken the photograph Lturungen picked up his rucksack and ran. I found him huddled in a corner of the cabin, his arms clasping his chest. The cold had grown too much for him. He had goose pimples even on his face. He was quivering with cold and his teeth were chattering audibly. It took several hot cups of tea and two large cakes to restore his normal composure.

By the end of our stay we seemed to have travelled the whole of London, and I was footsore and weary. Lturungen, however, was in considerable pain. We had enjoyed ourselves so much that I had forgotten he was a cripple.

The operation on Lturungen's foot was successful insofar as it restored movement to his ankle, and enabled him to walk more easily, but the wound took much longer to heal than we ever imagined. Before he left, Lturungen made two substantial purchases with money he had been donated by local schools. One was a pair of lightweight crutches to help him if his foot gave him trouble in the future; the other was a large suitcase in which he could keep all his worldly possessions when he got home. It upset me to think that so talented an individual with so much to give the world possessed so little of his own.

Lturungen was his own greatest worth. He had come to England destitute, yet he had the power to inspire the hearts and minds of many hundreds of people. However little he owned in the way of worldly goods he nevertheless still had himself — his individuality and the wealth of his personality. The dearth of worldly comforts had enriched him as a human being while we poor souls, who are so encumbered by our possessions, have little time for ourselves.

Parting was harder than Lturungen expected. When we parked at Heathrow Airport the tears rolled down his cheeks, but by the time his flight was announced he had regained his composure, shook my hand and departed without looking back. In a letter posted from Nairobi he reported that the flight had been very enjoyable, and that he had been treated with unaccustomed courtesy at Nairobi airport.

"You see," he wrote, "I was wearing the tie you gave me. The officials took me for somebody important and it made all the difference."

Although his foot had prevented him from participating in so much of Samburu life, Lturungen had made up for it by acquainting himself with every detail of his tribal customs and traditions. By the end of his three-month stay I realised I had acquired a rich store of knowledge about the Samburu. Come the following January it was therefore no surprise to find myself in Samburuland putting all the knowledge I had acquired into practice, as Lturungen's guest at Karaito's circumcision and warrior making ceremony.

CHAPTER FIVE

Facing the Elders

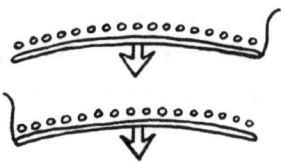

face-painting designs

"HOW INCONSIDERATE of you to bring this man to live in these terrible conditions!"

The elder threw Lturungen an accusing look. He was a big man with knowing eyes, a square and deeply lined face, a tinge of grey in the receding hairline, and earlobes pierced and stretched like mug handles. He sat on his haunches, *rungu* by his side, a red and yellow checked *nanga* over his shoulders and a loincloth which did nothing to hide his private parts. There was an air of authority about him like a judge presiding over a court. His mate, with a thin bird-like face and hawk eyes in a red *nanga* and a felt hat, was stretched out on a cow hide. Lying on his back, legs crossed and left arm draped across his forehead, he chimed in with "*Eh, eh*" in agreement.

Lturungen was caught off his guard; he hadn't expected this. "But he wanted to come here," he protested.

It was a hot day. We were sheltering from the worst of the midday heat under the 'Elders' tree, an extra-large acacia under which the senior members of the local villages sat and debated measures to regulate the day-to-day conduct of their communities. Although we were not reached by the direct rays of the sun, its conspirator the wind sought us out and seared us with passing eddies. It riffled through the sandy soil and created miniature dust-devils as it passed.

I looked around our little group. It was not a debating day.

Had it been so, twenty or thirty men would have been assembled under the branches of this venerable tree. Other than myself there were five representatives of three of the five age-sets of Samburu male society — the child, the junior elder and the senior elder. The warrior class and the fire stick elder were missing.

Lpiritian and Lturungen were the junior elders and Lmunyaki, their half brother, was the child. Lturungen was sensitive to criticism and had bridled at the unwarranted accusation lobbed at him by the senior elder not without reason. In his community he was something of an outcast. He had been to secondary school and that was against tribal laws. He was as yet unmarried, and as a junior elder that too was against tribal tradition. It was not his place to contradict a senior. Not that the elder was a judge. He had no authority to admonish him, for the Samburu, like the Maasai, decide such matters democratically through consensus by all the senior elders.

Lpiritian and Lturungen had smoothed the way for me to stay with them and to participate in the circumcision and warrior-making ceremonies — the two most important events in the Samburu life cycle. Karaito and his half brother Lobuka were both aged about twelve. The four year period of circumcision for boys was about to close and would not be resumed until a new age-set opened in ten years time. Lpiritian had decided to circumcise the boys now, even though they were a little under the age, rather than wait until their early twenties, by which time the operation would be more painful. The case for me to join them had been made convincingly, and there had been no hint of disapproval from the elders. It was a great privilege and one I much appreciated. But the situation had now taken a bizarre twist, these two old men seemingly supporting me in preference to their kinsman.

The Samburu are xenophobic. 'Welcome' is a word with no counterpart in the Samburu vocabulary. Yet 'Welcome' is a word which is overworked in Kenya; it reflects the openness of the Kenyan peoples. 'Welcome' is said in a thousand ways and with as

Lmunyaki listening to the Elders

many nuances: 'Welcome to our home'; 'Welcome' says the shopkeeper as you both enter and leave; 'Welcome' schoolchildren chant before they perform their play; 'Welcome' when you eat, when you drink, and when you are shown to your seat. It is a word for which the Samburu have never had a use.

Within the tribe everyone is welcome at any time, for food and lodging, help and support. All share whatever they have. They regard their lifestyle as complete, self-fulfilling and superior to others. They have no need of strangers and no particular wish to welcome them. Throughout the time I stayed with the Samburu no one cared a jot about my background, my family, how I lived or the country from which I came. No questions were ever asked. I was accepted for what I was, no more and no less.

Knowing all this, the old man's derogatory reference to their living conditions took me by surprise. I mused on his use of the word 'terrible', and concluded that his concept of acceptable conditions for a white man must have been based on hearsay originating from the two tourist lodges in the area, where pampered visitors enjoyed a style of luxury he could not imagine and would never experience.

My attention turned from Lturungen to Lpiritian. I could see that Lpiritian was not going to be drawn into an argument and he behaved as if he had not heard the elder. Lpiritian's skin was very dark, almost black. He had a deep forehead; his long eyelashes enhanced the softness of his eyes and his mild and open face and the shape of his mouth gave the impression that he was always on the verge of breaking into a smile. Although he had had to take on the mantle of head of the family at an early age, I could never imagine him beating his wife or his mother as those who command a Samburu household are prone to do when the females of the family offended them. There were occasions when I heard others taunting him for being so mild-natured, yet he did wield very considerable authority. When he ordered somebody to do something he did it quietly and compellingly. He considered carefully before he spoke. Without being in the least bit pompous he had a reserve and a dignity that a cabinet minister might have envied. Yet he had a fine sense of humour, and his mirth invariably expressed itself in a delightfully endearing chuckle. He inspired confidence, and he was one for whom I had the deepest respect.

For now, though, Lpiritian judged it diplomatic to take no part in the dispute. Since I was the cause of the argument, I felt I had no alternative but to intervene and rescue Lturungen from the situation. As I began to gather my thoughts, I realised with surprise how easily I had adapted to a blood and milk diet, supplemented by a little rice and cabbage or by *posho*. The brothers cooked this food for me from time to time for fear my constitution would not withstand the sudden change from a largely solid to an all-liquid diet. The heat too had not been a problem, and perhaps because of the drought there were relatively few flies.

What was so appealing to me here was the peace and tranquillity, the lack of hurry and the opportunity afforded to think, reflect and contemplate, and to be oneself. I could observe life rather than be driven by it, and by observing so I became more acquainted with myself as the observer. I re-established an identity which had become submerged in the endless current of action, sound and visual stimulation which sweeps us along during the normal course of our lives. Maybe it was because I now enjoyed this calm pool of contentment that I felt so much at home in this environment.

In defence of Lturungen I tried to say why I wanted to stay with the Samburu, and to explain in simple terms what it was that appealed to me. I chose my words carefully, trying to reduce complex concepts to ones that the elders could readily assimilate, but I could see I was making little headway. These old men simply did not understand; eyes glazed over and faces became expressionless. They had no concept of any life other than their own.

It brought to mind the anguish that Lturungen had expressed many times in his letters to me. He, who had travelled to England, had come home and talked about his experiences and shown his photographs to his mother and his family, and they simply stared at him in blank incomprehension. Once, when I had written to Lturungen about a problem we were having with a neighbour, his mother who could not envisage someone living in a permanent dwelling exclaimed, "Why doesn't the silly man just migrate to another place?"

"They don't understand me," Lturungen would wail. "Even a heap of dung would be more responsive. They laugh at me when I tell them the things I have done, and they say I am out of my mind. They can't believe what I tell them. They are not even interested in what I have to say. You can't imagine what it is like to have no one to talk to, no one to share these experiences with. When I come back home, my mind feels like it is shut up in a prison."

Here was a young man just out of his teens, caught between two cultures which were a world apart, yet he belonged to neither of them. Had he remained wholly within the tribe he would now have been in the prime of life, a respected junior elder, and the world — the Samburu world that is — would be at his feet. But the outside world offered few opportunities to those from pastoralist tribes. It was only now that I had come to live with Lturungen's family that I fully understood the dilemma which he faced and the trauma he was going through.

"In the old days the sign of ability was a spear and a shield. Today it is the exercise book and a pen," Jomo Kenyatta had said when he ruled Kenya, yet the system had failed Lturungen and many others like him. Then came the humility of being forced back into a tribal system he had tried to leave, and the ridicule which followed.

"So you wanted to better yourself, Lturungen. What have your great ideas done for you? We have goats; we have cattle; we have learned the skills of the warrior, and what have you got? Nothing, except a head full of useless knowledge."

My attention turned to Lmunyaki who observed from a respectful distance all that was going on. He had been given the day off from his usual task of tending goats. He was about eight years old, an intelligent boy with bright eyes, a long face, a flattish nose and an army of large white teeth which, when he smiled, burst out of his dark face like the sun coming out from behind a cloud. I looked at his slim, gracefully formed figure, and marvelled that he like all the other children thrived on a diet which consisted almost entirely of milk. He had walked the hour and a half from the *nkang* to spend the day with us, and dutifully ran errands for Lturungen, seemingly always smiling and obedient as he was obliged to be to somebody above his station.

Nkanyit — respect — dominates the world of the Samburu. It is the means by which the elders ensure codes of behaviour and morality are maintained. It pervades the conduct of the tribesmen and embraces even their eating habits, forms of address, sexual behaviour and the care of animals. It goes hand-in-hand with *lajii*, the hierarchical age-set system for men and boys which governs all their duties and responsibilities. An elder will talk to a married woman at a respectful distance. Strangers will always greet one another, approaching slowly and gradually, and asking after each other's family and livestock. A child will address an elder meekly, standing at a distance and waiting until called upon to speak.

At first I thought Samburu children must be terrified of me, such was their obeisance. It never occurred to me that I was considered venerable in their sight. Left to themselves, their gaiety was spontaneous and effervescent. They appeared to have no inhibitions and exhibited no fear. Life for them, when they were not involved in the serious business of tending livestock, was one long round of joy. As a grandparent would enjoy the company of grandchildren, so I would love to have participated in their fun. Instead, age and respect were insurmountable barriers. If I was to be accepted by these people I too had to conform to their standards of behaviour and respect.

Lmunyaki was lying on his stomach, feet in the air, his chin resting on the palm of his hand, listening intently. Unlike Lturungen, and in common with many Samburu children,

Lmunyaki would not attend school. His education was here in the village, absorbing the talk of those around him: the condition of the cattle; the effect of the drought; the punishment meted out to an elder for a misdeed — all this was enlarging his understanding of the governance of his people. In his play he was using hands, feet, eyes, nose, legs and arms in the rudimentary skills of survival — learning to use a spear, to run, climb, to make fire, to track animals, and to use a bow and arrow. Earlier, as a small child, he would have absorbed the stories and songs imparted to him by the older members of his family when they sat with him in the heat of the afternoon or around the fire at night. All these experiences were being stored up in his memory, a mosaic of facts, impressions, opinions, values and traditions on which he would draw in later life. In a society where there are few artifacts, no permanent buildings and where nothing is written down, it is this web of impressions and memories in the mind of every child which, as they grow up, ensures both the identity and the continuity of the tribe.

There was another dimension to Lmunyaki's education too, and that was the great book of nature. As he roamed the plains and forests or rested beside the river bank, he learnt to read the movement of the grass, the ripple in the water, the snapping twig, the flight of the bird, the tracks and scents of animals, the squawks and shrieks, the roars, snorts and howls and the cry of the hunted. He witnessed rutting, mating, birth, death and decay. Those harbingers of wisdom — reasoning, reflection and simple contemplation — had full sway and would eventually furnish him with the poise and a self-confidence which characterise the Samburu.

There is no gradual process of growing up in the Samburu tribe. Life advances in gigantic leaps as each stage in life is passed. A child is a child and treated as such, no matter what his age, until he is circumcised. This event can occur anywhere between the ages of thirteen and twenty five. Circumcision is in itself a test of a boy's courage and self control, and is the entrance exam to the university of warriorhood which follows, where his maturing body and mind are tried, tested and tempered through the fire of discipline, bravery, loyalty and respect until eventually he graduates as a junior elder, fully self-reliant, skilled in survival, husbandry and tribal law.

Lmunyaki now turned to doodling in the soil, but I fancied he still had an ear for the men as they talked. I wondered whether he ever gave any thought to his background. What were his origins? He had been too young to remember his father, and because the dead are never spoken of the chances were that he knew nothing about his grandfather. It was little wonder that the folk memory of the tribe did not go back far.

Like most of the tribes in East Africa the arrival of the Samburu in the area is relatively recent. In days gone by, Kenya was like a circus with men and animals constantly on the move, either avoiding enemies, being driven by adverse climatic conditions or hunting for food. They criss-crossed the plains and the Rift Valley, and as they did so new tribes pressed into this largely unpopulated territory from the west and north. With colonisation and the growth of settlements even the pastoralists have now become identified with particular tracts of land.

Until the white man arrived in Kenya, the Maasai ruled supreme. They believed God had created cattle only for them. They bludgeoned their way through the country from the arid lands of the north to the fertile plains of the south, increasing their herds by poaching livestock from those they encountered on their way. Elderly people living on the coast have told me how, as youngsters, they and their parents would hide up behind barred doors whenever the Maasai appeared in the vicinity, and stay there until they had moved on.

Yet the Maasai were never a homogeneous tribe. Clan warfare was rife. It seems the Samburu themselves originated from a break-away clan, preferring to remain in the north of the country while the rest of the Maasai pushed south. Perhaps that explains why they prefer the name Loikop to describe themselves rather than Samburu, which is of Maasai origin. The derivation of Loikop is unclear but it seems to mean those who are left behind, referring perhaps to their sojourn in the north.

Of Nilo-Hamitic origin, the Maasai and Samburu once inhabited the Nile basin. Then it seems they migrated up the Nile until they reached the hot and barren lands around Barangoi. The Samburu share the same language as the Maasai, but speak it much faster so that it rolls off the tongue like machine-gun fire. Many of their customs are similar but perhaps through intermarriage with neighbouring tribes they have achieved a separate identity. They are neither as arrogant nor as warlike as the Maasai although they share the same amazing self-confidence. They are also a great deal more relaxed and good-humoured. The Samburu are easily distinguished by their well-formed eyebrows and eyelashes which their cousins lack, and from the colour and pattern of the beads they wear. The Samburu always choose strong colours — black, white, bright red, deep orange and deep blue. I remember showing Lturungen a Maasai bracelet I had acquired. It was fashioned almost entirely from pale blue and gold beads.

"You'd never catch me wearing these colours," he said scornfully. "They are effeminate!"

By the time he is eight or nine, a Samburu boy will become responsible for herding goats. It is the first sign of his growing independence. He also begins to adopt the characteristic stance of the older men, standing on one leg, leaning on a stick with a *rungu* tucked between his legs. It is a stance reminiscent of the tribes living in the Sudan, as is the use of spittle as a blessing and is perhaps the strongest indication that the tribe had its origins in the north. Furthermore, although the method of circumcision is different, some aspects of the circumcision ceremony and also the hairstyles of the warriors and the use of wooden headrests as pillows are customs which bear a striking resemblance to those of ancient Egypt.

Over the course of time the Samburu have adapted well to the arid land they inhabit, but in recent years it is the drought rather than the imprecise dynamics of the modern Kenya and the associated intolerance of nomadic peoples which has brought them almost to their knees. Severe drought comes in cycles, bringing death to cattle in their hundreds and thousands. The wealth of an elder is measured in head of cattle and reflected in the number of wives he has. Many an elder has lost a fortune by the decimation of his herds in recent years. With them has gone his prestige in the tribe, his livelihood, and the main source of his food supply and basic commodities. Yet the women and children live on; there are hungry mouths to be fed and although the Samburu share all their possessions and will even give away their precious cattle in times of need, when all the herds are diminished sharing is of little avail.

By now the conversation had petered out and we sat under the tree in silence. The elder's attention was again focused on me. This time it was my turn to be controversial.

"So why do you cling to your traditions," I asked, "why are you content with this way of life? What is it that keeps you from moving forward with the rest of the Kenyan people?"

The old man thought for a little, poking his *rungu* in the ground. Then he turned and looked me full in the face. His reply was like a blast from an ancient scripture — as ancient as the ways of the tribe itself. A half memory, perhaps, from the days of the early prophets. This old man with his time-worn face and ragged attire was very wise.

"You see," he said, "when people like you look at a man you ask yourself 'What has he achieved? How wealthy is he? What position of importance does he enjoy? How much land or property does he own?' These are the outward things. Your vehicles, your buildings, even your clothes are outward things. With these you judge a man falsely.

"When we look at a man we ask ourselves 'How brave is he? How much respect does he command? How much wisdom does he have? How honest? How trustworthy? How reliable is he?' We see the man as he really is. That is why we care so little about the outer things of life, the things which are for show, and why we are content with our living conditions.

"Nkai is the only ruler, the only one with power. That is why the Loikop have no rulers or chiefs, no one person in a position of power. We share our wisdom as we share all things. That is also why the leaders of this nation laugh at our ways and regard us as little better than savages."

CHAPTER SIX

Water — *Nkare*

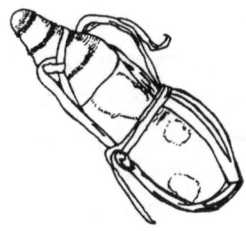

gourd for carrying water or milk

THE DAY AFTER I arrived at the *lorora* Lturungen suggested we went to see the cattle being watered. This was not a daily task as their hump-backed cattle can survive for several days without water. Goats and sheep are always grazed apart from the cattle; they were the responsibility of the young boys and young women who would return with them for a short rest during the noonday heat.

The cattle went further afield in search of pasture and stayed away all day. They were driven out of the *lorora* by the older uncircumcised boys before the sun was clear of the horizon. By then the boys had drunk their morning milk and hung a small container of water around the neck of one of their animals so that they would have something to quench their thirst during the heat of the day. All the men in the *lorora*, it seemed, helped to get the cattle on their way. The loose branches which formed the gates in the thorn hedge surrounding the encampment were opened up and the cattle driven out. Thereafter, the boys took over and remained in charge of the herds until they returned shortly before sunset.

On this particular morning the cattle remained in the *lorora* a little longer than usual before being driven off in the direction of the water. In the meantime the women busied themselves tying pack frames to donkeys. The frames were woven from wicker and string, and oval in shape like giant snowshoes. They were secured by ropes on either side of the animal after a cow hide had been placed over its back to prevent chafing. When not in use these frames were lodged vertically inside the hut (*ngajii*) to screen off sections of the interior. The children ran to collect gourds and plastic jerry cans in which drinking water would be transported, and these were lodged between the frames.

Some of the containers were a sorry sight, battered and badly split. I had seen the same thing on a Luyha farm in the west of Kenya. Then the water had been collected in old metal or plastic drums loaded onto a great oxcart. It came from piped springs a mile or more away. When we arrived with our creaking cart the younger children of the family joined the throng around the water supply and jostled each other for a place at one of the outlets. Those filling containers were watched intently by the others as the water neared the brim. It was an exercise in agility and cunning to see if you could out-manoeuvre your neighbour for a place under the pipe the moment someone turned away.

One second they were poised for action, the next there was a scramble for places. Sometimes it was achieved through sheer speed, sometimes by distracting the attention of the others at the critical moment, and occasionally by brute force. Even the smallest children grew bold with impatience, and I was amused to see one lad outwitted by a small girl who thrust both herself and her canister between his parted legs to beat him to the water supply just as he stooped to put his container under the pipe. Some of the drums had no lids and others leaked badly. The journey home lay along rough tracks and field boundaries, and by the time the oxen reached the farm half the precious load had been lost.

Charitable organisations have made great strides in bringing piped water to rural Africa, but a reliable supply of serviceable water containers is still a widespread need.

The cavalcade moved off from the *lorora* at a slow pace and we walked well clear of the enveloping dust. At times it almost obscured the cattle from view. On the way we were joined by Isaac, a friend of Lpiritian and Lturungen. An intelligent young man with a good command of English, he had a quiet manner and a face with finely chiselled features. Although obviously old enough to be a warrior he wore no beads and had short hair. I was curious until he explained that he too had been through school, and had been unable to find a job at the end of it. He had missed the opportunity to join in the activities of warriorhood and had returned to his family where, in contrast to Lturungen, he had been welcomed back as an able-bodied member of the community.

We walked on through the thin woodland and bush for half an hour or more, and then the cavalcade stopped and the dust subsided. Cutting through the trees ahead lay a dry watercourse or *lbaan*, as the Samburu call them. We dropped down a slope and on to the bed of the river below, and there ahead of us was the most enchanting pastoral sight.

The smooth surface of almost white sand ran like a ribbon between stony banks. At intervals of about ten yards there was a line of shallow wells some nine feet across dug in the sand. A warrior, knee-deep in each well, bailed water into long troughs made from hollowed-out tree trunks. Each had a carved wooden knob at the ends so that they could be carried from one well to another and heaved up to higher ground when the river was in flood. Groups of four or five cattle at a time were separated from the herd and led down to drink.

As they drew water and the cattle drank, so the warriors sang; not the throbbing petulant songs of warriorhood but something akin to a lullaby, their movements synchronising with the steady rhythm of their voices. They sang to calm the cattle and to encourage them to drink. Around each well waiting to lead the cattle back to the herd, young boys stood stork-like on one leg, balancing on staves or spears as is the Samburu fashion and along the bank knots of elders, gaunt and motionless in their *nangas*, watched intently as the animals were watered.

The brilliance of the sun reflected from the sand. The air was still; the heat of the day had not yet lifted the wind. Above, paper-white clouds drifted in the sky. The scene was one of penetrating harmony and peacefulness, the figures silent and observant, the unhurried movements of the cattle and the voices of the young men mingling and rising like incense in the clear dry air. It was a ritual of timeless simplicity and haunting beauty.

Dutifully, graciously, almost devoutly, the warriors drew out of that barren sand already hot from the sun the liquid that refreshes and sustains all living things. Here in stark reality was the earthly trinity on which life depends — sun, soil and water. Sun and soil these people had in abundance, but the availability of water determined the survival of the tribe and its prosperity. Little wonder that in the Samburu order of priorities after Nkai, the originator of all life, comes *nkare* which sustains both themselves and their beloved herds.

Those elders would know their stock and the characteristics of every animal as well as they knew their wives, and could recite the lineage of each one of them. They ran a discerning eye over their cattle in the mornings when they went out to graze, and again when they returned in the evenings. Frequently they would accompany them to their pasture, often paying more attention to their animals than they would spare for their women. Although goats, sheep and even camels contribute to the economy, it is the cattle which are the mainstay of Samburu life. Their cattle are to them as the reindeer is to the Lapp — two groups of people living at either end of the climatic extreme, both nomadic, and both dependent upon a single animal. In each case the herd is an investment in survival as well as a sign of personal wealth.

The wealth of a Samburu man begins at birth when his father presents him with a male calf. As he grows up the child cherishes this animal, and he will continue the bloodline throughout his life. It is the foundation of his herd and its progeny will eventually provide for bride wealth.

"Ten cows for a wife is a lot of money," I taunted Lpiritian, who had been married for only a couple of years. The drought had decimated his wealth and he had to borrow cattle to pay for his bride. He shook his head seriously.

"You see," he said, "it's not just a wife you are buying but also her childbearing potential."

So that was it, I thought. Samburu men really do regard their women as a mere vehicle for procreation.

Lturungen had claimed the boys' father really had loved his second wife, their mother. It was plausible, because whereas his first wife may well have been chosen for him by his father, his second would have been of his own choosing and she as likely as not could be the woman of his dreams. Nevertheless his love seemed to have been an exception. I had seen Lpiritian express little affection for his wife, Morissa, attractive though she was.

Once when we had been out on safari he arrived back at the *nkang* and greeted her with a single command *"Ndaa"* — food!

I castigated him, and demonstrated how I would have greeted my wife if I had been away for a few days. Both he and Morissa fell about in helpless laughter at the thought of kissing and hugging which to them seemed both ridiculous and unseemly.

The wealthier the elder, the more wives he can acquire. In Lpiritian's view a rich man was reckoned to have fifty or more cattle. His father's herd had far exceeded that number when he was alive. A man is respected for the number of cattle he owns, but is highly esteemed if he is also generous with them. A gift of a cow or a bull is the greatest gesture a man can make. Gifts of cattle occur at all the turning points in life; at birth, at circumcision for boys, and on marriage for girls. In the weeks before circumcision bands of initiates wander from village to village begging for cattle for meat. No elder would ever refuse such a request, even if his herd had dwindled to just a few head.

I stood and watched the riverbed for a long time. Was this

which I saw before me really happening at the close of the twentieth century? With all the sophistication of our towns and cities, here was a place where man was back at his roots making simple provision for his basic human needs. Some would claim, and indeed did, that these people had not yet started on the road of civilisation. To them I would question the definition of civilisation.

I conjured up in my mind a picture of Nairobi, or was it London, or Bombay, or indeed any great city in the world, and I recollected the poverty and squalor, the bondage of desperation and dejection, the greed, the avarice, the struggle for power and the ostentatious wealth of the few. Was this civilisation?

In this place the division between rich and poor was small; hardship was shared, and all came to the help of those in need. Here a man could walk proud and free and equal among his peers. It was only the lot of women which played on my conscience, and when I came to know the tribe better I came to realise that even their role, though wearisome, had its advantages.

After all the cattle had been watered, the donkeys had drunk their fill and the water containers were brimming, thorn branches were replaced round each well to prevent wild animals from breaking down the sides and fouling the water. Then the warriors slapped the rumps of their animals and the column began to move, the women and donkeys bringing up the rear. When they had departed at the same leisurely pace it was as if the process of life had stopped. The *lbaan* was desolate, silent in the heat of the sun. The wind was beginning to fill the hoof-prints with blown sand. Soon the only evidence of the morning's activity would be a few heaps of dung.

There were about a dozen of us left, mostly boys with no responsibility for livestock, together with Lturungen, Isaac, Karaito and myself.

As if to break the spell Lturungen said, "We ought to wash. I'll teach you the Samburu way."

He slipped off to a well and came back with a can of water. He took off his shoes and found a flat stone on which to place his injured foot. Then he stripped and washed by tipping a little of the water over his head. When that was clean he rinsed it, letting the water trickle down over his shoulders, chest and back which were washed next. And so on, until bit by bit he had worked his way down his entire body. The process was carried out with great concentration and thoroughness, and with the utmost gravity, and all was achieved with a single can of water.

To mark my arrival, Lturungen had acquired a bar of soap which for me was a welcome alternative to the sand usually used by the tribesmen. When it was my turn to wash a fresh can of water was fetched. I stripped and did the best I could to follow Lturungen's example. Seeing I was an amateur at this business, the spectators were liberal with their advice and took a keen interest in my performance.

I succeeded in doing my hair, neck, arms and chest to their satisfaction, alternately washing and rinsing, but failed miserably when it came to the area between the shoulder blades. To my surprise Lturungen stepped in and took over. We had looked after him with a great deal of loving care when he was recovering from his operation, and it was as if he were now returning the compliment. He took me back to childhood and being scrubbed down in the bath at home by a mother who didn't trust her youngster to do a proper job on his neck, his ears, and the small of his back. She made me stand in the bath to save her bending in just the same way as I was standing in the tropical sun, and her scrubbing was as relentless as that applied by Lturungen. Now some fifty years later it was a humbling experience to go through the same process, except that on this occasion instead of enjoying the privacy of a bathroom I was being observed by a dozen or so critical strangers.

Men from the age of puberty onwards are scrupulously discreet in front of girls and women, deftly covering themselves with their single *nanga* whether standing or sitting, but I quickly came to realise there was no such modesty in Samburu male company. Men regarded their bodies in a very matter-of-fact way. They were no more and no less than the means by which they could live and procreate in an earth-bound existence. Homosexuality, it seems, is non-existent.

I was intrigued to find that after circumcision Karaito took a real pride in showing me how well his wound was healing. An attitude perhaps understandable in a society where men and women live such separate lives but how different to Luyha tradition which is prudish in the extreme, and where even young children would think twice before running around naked. There bathing takes place in the privacy of a fenced-off bath place, squatting on the ground in front of a large bowl and splashing the water liberally over one's body with cupped hands. One feature was common to both traditions however, and that was the delicious warmth of the sun on one's body, and moreover that you had to stand around for only a few minutes before you were perfectly dry.

Throughout the exercise the audience had scrutinized my body from a respectful distance. It was not the colour of my skin that had caught the attention of the youngsters, nor were they surprised to see a man of my age uncircumcised. There were, after all, a number of coal-black Turkana who lived in the area. They are a tribe whose customs do not embrace circumcision.

"The problem," Lturungen explained, "is the hair on your body."

In most parts of Africa tribal people wear their hair short. Except in the case of warriors, long hair is associated with ne'er-do-wells and Lturungen assured me that he would need a licence in this part of Kenya before he could grow a beard. We had noticed how the Kenyan boys who had stayed with us in England habitually plucked the hair from under their arms and from their legs, and trimmed the hair on their heads. Small black whirls would appear everywhere — in the hand basin, the bath, underneath the bath mat, and in the carpets. This hair was adept at concealing itself and even after regular vacuum-cleaning a small cache would turn up unexpectedly months after our visitors had left.

Why, I wondered, did the presence of human hair trouble Africans? Why was it that for every important ceremony Samburu men and women shaved their heads? Did they, perhaps unconsciously, associate the presence of hair with the brutishness of the animals around them? Lturungen and his friends could give me no reason why they should feel this way.

Our ablutions over, there was still one item of toilet to be performed. Lturungen had continually reminded me how Nkai, in his wisdom, had provided for every Samburu need. There was iron ore in the mountains for their spears and knives, red ochre and clay in the ground for painting themselves and making pots, a huge range of herbs with medicinal properties, salt licks for cattle, plants from which they could make ropes and weave mats, honey for making mead, plants from which they could make snuff, thorn tree branches to protect their encampments, and so on. Providence had also ordained that the *sekotei* tree was a water-loving tree which grew along the *lbaan* and that was propitious because it was the tree from which toothbrush sticks or *nkike* were cut.

"Isn't it marvellous?" Lturungen remarked with approbation, "instead of having to look all over the place for a toothbrush Nkai has provided them just where we need them, right next to where we wash."

A *sekotei* grew within a few yards of where we stood. Isaac was quick to shin up into the branches and cut us some of the more succulent twigs from the top of the tree, and we cleaned our teeth at leisure as we trekked back to the *lorora*.

The longer I stayed with the Samburu the more I realised that washing was regarded as a ritual. Never a day passed without time being set aside for the solemn ceremony of cleansing the body. Some days, when we went on safari, we washed a second time on our return home.

Whereas a wash could be wonderfully refreshing and kept the body free from perspiration, it did little to keep the dust at bay. A wash and a stroll back to the *lorora* and our legs and arms were again covered with a thin film of reddish soil. Washing was not confined to the grown-ups; the men washing outside, the women in the privacy of the *ngajii*. Children washed regularly as well, and in order to save the precious liquid I saw mothers with young children fill their cheeks with water and wash their babies by squirting water on them from their mouths.

The more I took part in this ritual, the more it seemed to me that washing not only cleansed the body but appeared to be an intuitive reaction, perhaps symbolising the liberation of the psyche from the confines of the earth. The Samburu do not believe in spirits in the way many of the other tribes do, but the power of Nkai, the Supreme Being, was often in the forefront of their minds. Although they never expressed it in as many words, washing was for them virtually a sacramental experience. Seen in this light, St John baptising in the wilderness was performing but an extension of a basic human realisation.

Sometimes we washed at wells, sometimes from a can of water drawn from the domestic supplies in the *lorora*. On occasions we washed in the Wuaso Ngiro, now running extremely low in some places and dried up altogether in others. The crocodiles had holed themselves up in the banks to await the rains. Children took their place instead, playing boisterously in the shoals. One stretch alongside the Samburu lodge had dried out completely and no longer provided security from wild animals. I asked Lturungen how safe it was for tourists if lion and buffalo could walk across the bed and into the lodge grounds.

"Oh they wouldn't do that," he assured me. "You see, the baboons regard that bank as their territory and they would attack in such large numbers as to drive the animals away."

Where the river was still running we could stand knee-deep in the brown liquid to wash and then dry ourselves on the bank, while others came in twos and threes to perform the same task. Lturungen remarked that the Samburu regarded people from other tribes as dirty because they washed themselves so infrequently. I wondered what he thought about some of the youngsters he had met in England, where a lick and a promise so often suffices.

After the circumcision and warrior making ceremonies, when we moved back to the *nkang* from the *lorora* we found the wells to be in a poor state, and I wondered whether they would have to be dug deeper. Digging and maintenance falls to locally appointed families or else sub-clans of the tribe. When the rains come and the rivers flow these depressions are filled with sand and have to be dug afresh once the water subsides. In some parts of the country they can be very deep indeed, requiring five or even six warriors working as a team, handing up water to the surface in buckets made of giraffe skin. Then the work can be long and laborious, and calls for a great deal of stamina.

Towards the end of my stay I longed to see the clouds gather, the rains come and these dried river beds flow with water. It seemed inconceivable that it could ever happen in such a parched land.

"When it rains," Lturungen said, "the children run out of their huts and dance around for joy as the storm breaks, and play on mud slides wherever they can find a suitable slope."

It was not until we had returned from the *lorora* that I met Buni, Lturungen's other brother, midway in age between Lpiritian and Lturungen. He was very different from the other two, darker than Lturungen, with a lean and rather mean-looking face, a mouth reminiscent of a clown's, and prominent ears. He gave the impression of being thin rather than slim, and possessed a chuckle which fell uneasily between being scornful and merry. Later I came to know him to be both autocratic and individualistic. For all his traits I had reason to be grateful to him, as it was he who had given Lturungen the spear to bring to England as a gift for me.

It was the middle of the day and very hot. Buni sat under the trees on the edge of the *lbaan* surrounded by his herd of goats, which his wife Nasaba and Lmunyaki had driven back from pasture. He had a few words of English, and with my few words of Maa we managed a simple conversation. As we sat and talked he picked up a long acacia thorn and reaching for my right ear, thrust it through the lobe, watching attentively for a reaction. There was none.

It was a most extraordinary thing to do to someone you had just met, but somehow I managed to continue the conversation as if nothing was happening, despite the discomfort. Then he withdrew the thorn and tossed it away unconcernedly. Afterwards, when I had had time to reflect on the incident, I thought maybe it was his way of protesting that I had not got pierced ears, or perhaps he was just testing my mettle. Whatever the motive we nevertheless became the best of friends.

Buni was unforgiving of Lturungen both for having gone to school instead of progressing through warriorhood, and for remaining unmarried. To him, Lturungen's injured foot was irrelevant. Whereas their father had decreed before his death that Lturungen could marry outside the tribe, he had chosen a Turkana as a husband for his daughter Ngalina, and had promised a daughter of each of two Samburu friends as wives for his sons, leaving the choice to them. One of the girls, Morissa, was just a little younger than Lpiritian and it was she he took as a wife. The other, Nasaba, can have been only six or seven years old when she was promised in marriage. Either Buni or Lturungen was obliged to marry her as there was no gainsaying a father's wishes, even after his death. There had been an argument between them since Lturungen, with authority to marry outside the tribe, resolutely refused to have anything to do with her. So Buni had married her when she reached the tender age of twelve.

Ngalina, poor girl, had fared little better. She was married a year without conceiving, and then her husband died of tuberculosis. Ngalina was then just sixteen. Samburu laws forbid a widow to remarry although she is permitted to entertain boyfriends, any ensuing children being brought up as part of the mother's family. As a sort of consolation for her misfortune,

Ngalina had been given her half brother, Lmunyaki, to bring up through childhood.

Buni still treated his wife as a child, and beat her when she displeased him. It was a blessing the girls got on so well together. It seemed as if Morissa, Ngalina and Nasaba were an inseparable threesome, and it was evident how much support little Nasaba got from this arrangement.

On the day I met Buni he was feeling off-colour. The heat coupled with the prolonged drought increases the micro-organisms in the drinking water, and tummy upsets among the Samburu were becoming prevalent. Some of the wells were now bright green and the water undrinkable. A new small well had been dug near the *nkang*, and I watched the girls spend a whole afternoon painstakingly collecting the water mugful by mugful as it welled up out of the sand. In a fit of temper Buni sent Nasaba and Lmunyaki out in the heat again with the goats while he lay down and rested. Later he drank a concoction made from acacia bark soaked in water which the Samburu use as a stomach medicine, and fell asleep until evening.

Lturungen and I took the opportunity for a rest, lying on our cow hides in the seclusion of the *lbaan*. I remember these afternoons with a great deal of pleasure. They inspired a feeling of dreamy contentment. The trees on either side of the riverbed were still green from an underground water source and gave welcome shade. The white sand stretched as far as the eye could see in one direction; in the other direction it was quickly obscured by a bend. The sandy banks of this narrow *lbaan* reached up to the tree roots and the trees themselves formed a green avenue in either direction, in places the highest branches almost meeting across the watercourse. There was no sound except for the sigh of the breeze in foliage from time to time, the buzz of flies and the bells of a couple of camels browsing in the distance, their mouths easily reaching the foliage reserved for them and which they plucked delicately, the branches being too high for cattle or goats to reach.

As if knowingly improvident an errant thought asked timidly

and almost inaudibly "Are you lonely in the vastness of this land beyond the reach of conventional living?"

I thought of the mercenary life I had left behind, of the blizzard of paper drifting from office to office, the tumult of figures, crucial today, inconsequential tomorrow, and the spewing, spawning data systems we are wedded to. I recalled the financial and political pressures under which I laboured, and the ceaseless demands of the punters.

The tyranny of business was banished from this hallowed land. I was lackey to no one. I was free as the birds of the air and the beasts of the plains. No longer did any person or machine intrude on my thoughts or intervene in my freedom to walk, sit, sleep.

I laughed at the audacity of such a question. How could anyone be lonely when he held court in his own kingdom?

CHAPTER SEVEN

Night — *Nguariye*

little Samburu boy

THE NOISIEST PART of the Samburu day is the night. In the daytime all except the youngest animals are out at pasture. The women busy themselves with their daily chores and when these are over they sit and talk laconically. In the heat of the day the elders roll up in their cow hides and lie in the shade of trees in almost complete silence, the only sound being the soughing wind and the occasional shouts of children playing. Then as the great orange sphere of the sun drops towards the horizon and the rasping heat dissipates to a soothing warmth, activity in the *lorora* is renewed and the livestock turns homeward. Cows, goats, donkeys, camels and dogs all come back through the gates in the surrounding thorn hedge to spend the night in the safety of the encampment.

This sudden movement of people and animals, the thundering hooves, the shouts and whistles of the drovers and the lowing and bleating of the driven comes upon the *lorora* so quickly that it is like stepping out of the tranquillity of Westminster Abbey and into the confusion of Parliament Square at the end of a working day. It is the Samburu rush hour.

In the *lorora* the cattle wandered freely, only the calves, goats and their young being penned up. The flurry of activity would slowly subside, the animals settle down and the boys make for their huts for their evening milk. The tropical darkness descends quickly. It comes like a warm, velvety blanket, smothering the sounds of the animals and quelling human activity.

Sitting out under the huge expanse of the firmament scattered with thousands of stars undimmed by the lights of human habitation was one of the delights of my time with the Samburu. Here and there in the darkness a fire outside one *ngajii* or another would suddenly blaze, sending up a shower of sparks as wood was thrown onto the embers, the glow lighting up the whites of the eyes of those around it, the light of the flames playing on the brass ornaments which adorned the women. Now the air was still and cool, the flames leapt heavenward and as if in deference to the subduing darkness, people talked in hushed tones, the murmuring around each fireplace like the hum of bees in the hive. Even the children were silent. They would sit quietly by the fire exhausted from the heat of the day, the smaller ones falling asleep where they sat, and one by one being lifted gently into bed.

Somewhere between ten and eleven in the evening people would drift into their huts and prepare for sleep, the embers of the fire inside guiding their way. I was familiar with the intense silence which was like our rural home in England, and the rhythmic breathing of those around me soon induced drowsiness.

All would go well until the small hours. Then, as if coerced by the spirits of the plains, the animals became subjected to a form of devilment. Often it began with the donkeys picking a fight. All of a sudden one of them would squeal as if it had been kicked. You would hear them career around, followed by stamping hooves and peals of braying, and then more squealing. At other times it would be a few giddy heifers or steers frightened by fireflies. Fireflies have a habit of flying at an altitude which corresponds to the eye level of standing cattle. The tiny ball of light winging its way silently through the night frightens them.

It takes only two or three animals to stampede for the rest to follow. The whole herd would shift uneasily and then break into a run, with much snorting and thumping of hooves. I would lie awake, expecting them to charge the *ngajii* at any minute, its frail walls collapsing under the bulk of their bodies, but fortunately it never happened. This liveliness was not confined to the animals inside the *lorora*. The same wakefulness was shared by those in the wild. In the distance you might hear the throaty roar of a lion or the whooping of a hyena as it raised its head to serenade the moon.

This devilment undoubtedly extended to warriors. In the lead up to circumcision and warrior-making, they assembled at the *lorora* in large numbers. Like the animals, they seemed to need little sleep and wandered about half the night. They would frequently burst into song and then dance into the early hours. As often as not a group of them would then converge on the *ngajii* and settle down outside in conversation. It was not the conversation which disturbed one's night-time rest so much as the thunderous shaking of cow hides before they sat on them, and the thud and clanking of spears laid against the roof.

When we left the *lorora* and went back to reside in the *nkang* the night was punctuated by the groaning and belching of the camels belonging to the next-door family, and the hollow clank of their large wooden bells every time they shook their heads.

On one occasion I was woken by howling and a tremendous bleating of goats. Lpiritian, who was sleeping next to me, suddenly leapt up and rushed through the doorway, holding his *nanga* around his waist. Pandemonium broke out for a while, and I wondered what on earth was going on. Some of the sounds were violent as if animals were under attack. I could hear Lpiritian and Buni and one of the neighbours shouting in agitated tones above the noise. Eventually Lpiritian returned, breathing heavily, and sank back onto his cow hide.

In the morning I asked him what had happened. "Hyenas," he said, "hyenas got through the stockade and into the goat pen. We had to chase them out. Fortunately none of the animals was seriously injured. We caught them just in time."

Lpiritian recalled how only a few months before, a herd of elephant had broken into the *nkang*. Thorn hedges are no obstacle to them. By the time the menfolk had emerged, the elephants were within a few yards of the huts. Had they taken fright and charged the whole encampment, inhabitants and livestock could all have been crushed to death. The Samburu make a lethal poison from a plant they call *ltulelei*. It is so poisonous that one arrow will fell the largest elephant immediately and kill it within minutes. The fleshy leaves and fruits are boiled in the open in pots set aside for the purpose. Care is taken to avoid inhaling the fumes. When the mixture thickens and turns black it is cooled, and the poison applied to the tips of arrows by means of a stick.

Even amongst the most well-regulated Samburu, nefarious activities take place at night and, because there had been a number of irate husbands applying this poison to suitors with fatal effects, the elders had banned its manufacture in this particular area. Knowing this, and faced with imminent danger, I wondered what they had done to save themselves.

"Well," explained Lpiritian, "you know we have a tradition of never allowing the fire in the *ngajii* to go out. There are good reasons for that. First, it is a long and laborious task to rekindle a fire by rubbing two sticks together, and secondly fire is an excellent protection against animals. We quickly revived the embers and threw burning sticks at the elephants. Even an elephant is frightened of fire and fortunately they moved off at a fast pace the way they had come. After that we stoked up the fires outside and kept watch for the rest of the night. Once frightened like this, they would be unlikely to return."

In the days leading up to the warrior-making ceremony excitement in the *lorora* ran high. The boys who had recently been circumcised, the *laibartak*, were eagerly awaiting their elevation to the glamorous and carefree life of warriors, and the existing warriors were anxious to show off their prowess. They gathered round the campfires in high spirits regaling the youngsters with tales of bravery and fortitude with youthful zest. They were joined by a number of firestick elders, the next but one *lajii* in line. They had abandoned their carefree warriorhood some years ago, but looked back on those days with nostalgia. There were invariably more round our fire than the others because of the attraction of the *mzungu* in their midst.

One evening, when the story-telling fell into a lull, I suggested they sang. The idea was taken up with alacrity. It was decided they would sing the 'joke' song. It was competitive, each singer taking turns to narrate at high speed a string of preposterous activities he had engaged in during the day. The Samburu are fast speakers in normal circumstances. This was a contest in oral dexterity and imaginative narration. One competitor began in a singsong voice until another felt he could outdo him, and chipped in with an even faster and more farfetched performance. And so it went on, the rest of the company contributing a drone accompaniment until at last it ended in helpless merriment and good-hearted banter as to who had been the winner.

Another evening when the atmosphere was less boisterous, an elder led a blessing ceremony. It was a catalogue of things brought before Nkai to be blessed, and lasted a full twenty minutes. Goats, cattle, knives, tools, children, wives — all were included in the recital. The elder intoned with the rhythm of a railway train — diddly dum, diddly dum, diddly diddly dum — and in between each phrase everyone chanted 'Nkai' which, as speed increased, was truncated to 'Hai', and lightly clenched and released their fists as they did so.

Nkai, omniscient, omnipotent and omnipresent, pervaded every facet of Samburu life. His blessing was invoked in daily tasks, at the conclusion of elders' discussions and at every important event and ceremony within the tribe. His presence was recognised as being in every living thing, but as in the Old Testament, when you wanted to be close to him you sought him in the peace and isolation of the mountains. In obeisance to Nkai the doorway of every hut in the *lorora* faced the nearest mountain, as did the roasting pits used during the warrior-making ceremonies, and in times of great need or at the commencement of a major tribal event the mountain top served as the Samburu altar for the sacrifice of animals.

Perhaps out of reverence, the Samburu were reticent regarding their relationship with Nkai. Only Lturungen, with whom I seemed to share some sort of spiritual rapport, was prepared to reveal his innermost feelings. He was fastidious in saying his prayers silently, morning and evening, and also said grace before he ate although this may have been a practice adopted from school. He also prayed when he walked, because it lessened his awareness of the pain in his foot.

"The Maasai do not believe in life after death. That is the biggest difference between our tribes. Many white people claim the Samburu don't either, but that is not true. They say this because we don't bury our dead unless they are very young or very old and respected, but leave them on the ground to be eaten by wild animals. They say it too because we never talk about the dead after they leave us. But you know, we are a practical people. Our passage on earth is short. We take every day as it comes. We do not concern ourselves unduly with the past or the future, only with the importance of living now. When people die they are no longer part of our lives. They are living their own lives away from us. That is sufficient."

I knew exactly what Lturungen meant. The British found that when they put the Maasai in prison they often died through their inability to foresee a time when they might be released. I experienced something similar with Lturungen a year or two later, in trying to help him find a job. He simply could not imagine his situation could change, that good fortune could shine on him and that he might one day be able to earn a living in the world outside. The acceptance of things as they are is common in Africa, but is particularly pronounced amongst the Maasai and the Samburu. To some extent it explains their fearlessness. Fear is, to a large extent, premeditated, and premeditation does not usually enter their thought pattern. I marvelled that a people who could be so self-assured, so brave and so independent, could at the same time lack the dimension of hope, of aspiration and of anticipation. And yet, given their harsh, inhospitable and unyielding environment, they were some of the most contented people I have met.

Despite Lturungen's insistence that they didn't think about the dead, I knew in his heart he longed for his father, the only person he had been able to turn to for guidance and advice during his troubled childhood, the one who had consoled and encouraged him. He was never likely to forget him, but would cling to his memory for the rest of his life. When he spoke of him, it seemed he withdrew into himself. His joie-de-vivre was dimmed, his eyes no longer sparkled, and he lost the strength in his voice. Perhaps because I had come to know him so well, I became intuitively aware of his feelings. On occasions when I had seen him put down by other Kenyans who believed they were of a superior tribe, he would bristle with indignation. His eyes grew as cold as steel, his face hardened, and his anger was pricking and uncomfortable as if he were radiating little arrows of static electricity. Yet when he was happy, as he mostly was, he became a magnet drawing others to himself, attracted by the warmth of his personality and his self-assurance.

The loss of his father was made worse in that of all the sons and daughters he was the only one who did not come to his deathbed and who never bade him farewell. Seemingly unaware of his attachment to his father, the family did not recall Lturungen from boarding school. They had felt it was better for his studies to continue undisturbed. In his view it was an unforgivable thing to have done, and it rankled still. When the news of his father's death eventually reached him, he was beside himself with grief for days and it was weeks before he could open a school book again.

That was some four years before he met us. When our paths first crossed he was tempted to treat us as surrogate parents. It would never have worked. If we were to give him the encouragement and support he needed, and to teach him to stand on his own feet we needed to treat him as an equal, not as a son. Besides, when a Samburu comes of age he discusses nothing personal with his mother and seeks the companionship of his age-set rather than his father. Despite the differences in age, it was not so difficult for him to regard me as a half brother. Our fathers were of the same age, and as the first-born of the first wife his eldest half brother was not far short of my own age.

The Samburu believe unquestionably in the power of the curse. It is the ultimate sanction. The elders are responsible for instilling *nkanyit* between husband and wife, between children and parents, between peers, between age groups and even between clans and sub-clans. It is so effective that petty crime is virtually unknown. When someone transgresses, the elders meet and decide on the form of punishment to be meted out. Every decision is required to be unanimous, and it may take days and occasionally weeks before unanimity is reached. The values and norms evolved by the Samburu over hundreds of years, together with the discipline enforced by the elders ensure that everyone pulls together to preserve the tribe in the face of the most remarkable odds.

One evening, sitting out under the night sky we saw a huge fire in the distance. At a time when the drought had reduced the herds to a level barely capable of sustaining the tribe, an elder had been ordered to slaughter and roast one of his precious cattle, and to share the meat with everyone around as punishment for his conduct. The matter had been debated all day long before the outcome was agreed. The sentence was acted upon immediately, and only if the offender had refused to comply might a curse have been used.

I turned to Lturungen. "Do you really believe in the power of the curse?"

"Do you believe in the power of blessing?" came the reply.

"Of course."

"Then if you believe in blessings, you are saying you also believe in curses. We live in a world of opposites. You cannot have one without the other. Curses are essential to us because, you see, being nomads we have no prisons. A curse is never placed on anyone lightly. You have to believe in the need for the curse in just the same way as you have to believe in the need for a blessing. In either case, it must be done with all sincerity otherwise it is ineffective. Neither can it be done in anger. But even if a curse is sincerely given and the offender is innocent, no harm will come to him. A curse must also fit the crime. The curse of death is rarely given. In the end Nkai is the final arbiter. He is lord of all, both blessings and curses, as well as those he has appointed to deliver them."

In the glow of the firelight, I caught sight of an impish grin on his face. "You know," he continued, "think of all the money you could save in England if you sentenced people with a curse. You wouldn't have to build and maintain any prisons, and the prisoners could be out in the community doing a useful job of work!"

We laughed, yet I was not altogether convinced.

"But have you seen a curse work?"

Lturungen considered for a moment. "I remember an occasion when I was about ten or eleven years old. There were several families living in our *nkang*. One of them had a boy of about my age who was wild and unruly. He disobeyed both his father and the elders. No one could remember another boy like him. He was an embarrassment to his family and his father was filled with shame. One morning not long after we had got up, his father asked him to carry out some duties for him. The boy blankly refused, and what is more he hurled a string of abuse at his father.

"Everyone was quite shocked. This was more than the old

man could stand. He had his own good name to maintain and that of his family, so he called everybody together and addressed the boy, saying '*Layieni lai*' (my son), 'if you are still alive when the sun is past its zenith and the shadows begin to lengthen, then you are not my son at all.' It was a very serious thing to say, and especially when a father says it of his son. That day everybody in the *nkang* was subdued, but being young and with our thoughts filled by many things we soon forgot about the episode.

"Later in the morning that boy and another friend and I decided to go off to cook some food. Because of my bad foot it was decided that I would be the one to light a fire while the other two went in search of firewood. I started to rub two sticks together in the way we make fire, and when the fire was burning nicely my friend came back with his firewood. The other boy had gone further into the wood looking for sticks. We had been together only a few minutes before we heard a kind of strangled cry. We left everything and ran to where the sound came from.

"There was the boy lying dead on the ground. We could see the pug-marks of a lion all round his body, and we saw where a paw had been placed on his neck. He must have surprised the lion. It had knocked him to the ground and put a paw on his neck until he suffocated, and then it had walked away. We were terribly shocked and ran back to the *nkang* sobbing."

"And what was the time?"

"It was just before midday."

Although Lturungen was convinced of the power of curses, it was not until he ran into a spot of bother at primary school that he became convinced of the power of the *laisi*, the men of the tribe who claimed to be able to find lost things and to bring good or ill luck. He had lost his pen. Although he had searched everywhere he could not find it. He had no money to buy another one, and so he was unable to write up his class notes. That had got him into trouble with his headmaster.

Knowing no other solution to his problem, Lturungen plucked up courage and went to seek the help of one of these

Early morning: cattle leaving for pasture

Karaito sterilising milk gourds

Ngalina

Morissa

Buni with his goats

Blowing the kudu horn (Sabachi in the background)

soothsayers who lived near the school. The *lais* assured him that it was well within his powers to find the pen.

"Do you know a boy named John?" he asked.

At first Lturungen said he didn't, but then he remembered there was an older boy at the school of that name whom he didn't know very well.

"You will remember he was around one day when you were playing with your friends at the back of the dormitory. He has your pen. Ask him for it, and he will give it to you."

Back at school Lturungen approached the boy, who denied having the pen. Lturungen was in a quandary. Was he to believe the *lais* or the boy? He hadn't the nerve to go back to the *lais* and tell him he had made a mistake, and he was afraid to tackle the boy again in case he beat him up. Yet he desperately needed that pen. Eventually he overcame his fear and approached the boy once more.

On the third time of asking John confessed, "Yes, you are right. I do have a pen which is not mine. I found it on the ground near the dormitory. I didn't imagine it was yours. How did you know I had it?"

Lturungen then told him about the advice he had received from the *lais*. The boy returned his pen immediately.

Lpiritian's work at the tourist lodge took him away from his wife Morissa for weeks at a time, so while he was on holiday he made a point of spending the evenings with little Alberto, his son. Alberto was an impressive child by any standards. He shared his father's dark skin, the same deep forehead and the same gentleness. All his actions were carried out slowly and deliberately which seemed strange in a child so young. Alberto's younger stepmother had a daughter who was of a similar age. She was frustrated by his docility, and on more than one occasion in childish play took a stick to beat a reaction from him. But his only retaliation was the tears which trickled down his cheeks when the pain got too much for him. His round enquiring eyes and his impressive gaze were more suited to a sage than a babe.

It was delightful to see father and son together. They adored each other's company. Lpiritian, Lturungen, Karaito and the ever-smiling half brother Senene and I would sit round the fire at night in conversation on our little round four-legged stools — the only furniture possessed by the Samburu, while Lpiritian played endlessly with Alberto. He loved to be tickled or flung over his father's knee, or stood on his shoulders and then swept to the ground in those strong supportive arms. He chuckled with delight, and like any healthy child, begged for more. Sometimes Lpiritian sat and danced him between his knees, singing to him the songs of childhood — the same songs he would sing to the goats and sheep when he was old enough to take them to pasture. These little lilting ditties were the means by which the Samburu communicated with their animals, whether herding or milking them. In just the same way as the warriors sang to the cattle to encourage them to drink their fill, so this singing calmed the animals and encouraged their milk yield.

Almost all Lpiritian's meagre salary was spent on the family. However, over the years he had managed to set enough aside to purchase his pride and joy — a ghetto blaster from which he was inseparable. It was an incongruous sight to see him clutching this large black object to his slim black body in the midst of the dust and dung of the *lorora*. Through their contact with the lodge and school respectively, both brothers had developed an ear for pop music. They were alone in their taste. It had no appeal for the warriors or the other young people who regarded all music other than their own with total disinterest.

When I made some recordings of the singing accompanying the warrior-making ceremonies, I lent one of the tapes to Lpiritian. Almost immediately he was besieged by incredulous tribesmen marvelling that this machine which, up until then, had held no interest for them but could now sing their own music. Thereafter Lpiritian was in great demand, and every time a new item was recorded the warriors demanded a playback, not just for the joy of hearing their own voices but also to make a critical analysis of their performance, recognising individual voices, chiding those who were out of tune or who entered a part song late, and praising those who excelled in their singing.

One clear, still evening when the clouds were passing across the path of an almost full moon, throwing the *lorora* alternately into pools of darkness and crescendos of light, Lpiritian sat and idly flicked through the wavebands as we talked. Then, caught up in the thread of conversation, his attention wandered from the radio and he set it on the ground. For a moment there was silence and then an orchestra, which could have been a million miles away or on another planet began to play the Romance from the Eine Kleine Nachtmusik. Serene notes on shimmering skeins wafted into the night.

Their beauty shattered my composure. It supplanted the joy and the satisfaction of mind I had acquired through living with the Samburu. It distorted the images and impressions of the time I had spent in this small corner of Africa. It disorientated my thoughts and memories. It threatened to drag me out of the dream of belonging and contentment I had experienced since coming to the *lorora*, and in which I still slumbered. I observed the dung at my feet. I recalled the taste of blood in my mouth, the slaughter of animals and I stared at the humble stick and mud hut in which we lived, lit in the flickering light of the fire. As the strains melted into the silence of the moon, they seemed to be tugging my heart and soul in opposite directions.

A tiny niggling thought began to develop in the back of my mind. "How much longer," it was saying, "how much longer can you live with these people in these surroundings before you succumb through yearning for all those things of beauty you are missing from your other existence?"

I experienced a moment of panic or fright — I am not sure which. What was I doing here, a tiny speck of humanity in this vast plain? Nothing but dried trees and grass, rock, boulders and sand. Only the little thorn fence stood as protection against the lion and the rhinoceros, the elephant and the leopard roaming in the darkness. The remoteness was unnerving. There was no possible means of communication with the outside world unless I took to my feet and hoofed it through that intimidating wilderness which even the boys were wary of venturing into after nightfall. The music, full of poise and 18th-century elegance, was the only tenuous, fleeting link I had. The music had no meaning for the boys and I doubt whether they were aware of it.

"Roger, what's the matter? Are you all right?" Lpiritian had been regaling the others with a story which had given them cause for laughter, and they had noticed my solemn face.

"Why of course. I was just thinking about something else." The music faded and I was back in the firelight, drawn into the companionship of these young people. I beheld their comeliness and self-possession. I looked up at the spangled heavens and at Orion just above the horizon, the same Orion I gazed upon from the garden at home. My same mind was touched and uplifted by the cry of the bird, the roar of the lion and the harmonies of Mozart. Our world, *the* world, is within us, complete and perfect. If we experience fear or loss or disorientation, is it not because we have momentarily lost ourselves? Thus reassured, I relaxed again in these now familiar surroundings.

It was not until we went to live at the *nkang* at the conclusion of the warrior-making ceremonies that I realised at first hand the depth of deprivation and suffering experienced by Lturungen. An unmarried elder was almost unheard of in Samburu society, with the exception of those few who may have exhibited fear while being circumcised, and who would be ostracised by the tribe. Then marriage would be out of the question except, perhaps, to a widow. When at the *lorora* the boys had cooked rice for me, Lturungen could not share it because there were women around who might see him eating. But there were often occasions when we would be out on safari in the company of young men of his own age and he could hide away with them and eat food in the certainty that he would not be observed by a female.

At the *nkang* there was no escape. Women were around all

the time fetching water, collecting firewood and milking the animals. The only opportunity he had to eat was late in the evening when everybody had retired to bed. Then Buni or I would accompany him so that there was someone for him with whom to share the food. This rigidly adhered-to custom reflected the Samburu tradition of sharing and ensured that when food was scarce no one went without. The only exception to this rule I ever heard about was when an animal was killed single-handed in the bush. Then, and only then was it permissible to light a fire and roast and eat the meat on one's own.

How Lturungen managed to get through the days with no more than water I shall never understand. The thought of me accompanying him into the bush late at night instead of curling up on my cow hide upset him greatly. The procedure he had to adopt was not straightforward. Being unmarried, he was not allowed to own a cooking pot. This first had to be 'stolen' from one of the *ngajii* as did water, without anyone seeing him, and it always created some tension before he aimed for the same spot down beside the *lbaan*. There was a clump of saplings in the midst of which he had created a small fireplace. This was his kitchen. Maize meal and fat were hidden nearby. When the fire was nicely burning he would fill the cooking pot with water and maize, and when it was cooked, add the fat. The resultant *posho* was then carried a few feet away to where two parallel tree trunks lay alongside the bank of the *lbaan*. This was his dining room. It was here that he would fall on his food, for by that time he was ravenous. This arrangement worked well when there was a moon. At other times it was extremely difficult to find one's way, and more than once I gouged a lump out of my head through walking blindly into a low-growing acacia branch with its murderous thorns.

When Buni joined us I could never be sure whether he came out of concern for his brother, or merely because it was a means of getting another meal. At times he scolded Lturungen unmercifully for remaining unmarried and causing so many difficulties. When this happened, all Lturungen's bonhomie shrank into himself. He became silent and withdrawn. It was as if Buni were a cat, and Lturungen a little mouse cowering in the corner. Lturungen never dared to mention to his brothers the effect the pain of his foot had had on his bodily sensations, and because of it the effect it would have on his married life. Nor could he ever hope to make them understand he had determined to marry only if he could find a woman he could genuinely love. Neither brother could comprehend his intransigence when it came to marriage. Why couldn't he pick on any eligible girl and just marry her to get himself out of this terrible predicament? As Samburu men lived such separate lives from their womenfolk, he would have the freedom to spend as much time away from her as he pleased.

It was easy to understand their exasperation with him, and I couldn't blame Buni for his uncompromising attitude. It made me appreciate what a prison Lturungen was holed up in, bound by a crippled body, uncompromising tribal laws and moral and spiritual scruples. At times my heart cried out to him, longing to help him by sharing the agony of his suffering, for while the Samburu are exemplary in sharing food and possessions they had yet to teach me a way of sharing the things of the mind.

Lturungen still had two more hurdles to clear after he had eaten his food. The cooking pot which he had stolen had to be cleaned and returned to its owners in such a way that they would not know it had been used. Then, because he was single, he was forbidden to sleep in the dwelling of a young married couple. This meant that, although there was room enough in both Lpiritian's and Buni's homes, he had to search for accommodation elsewhere. I understood now his deep despair on that fateful day in England when his friends had written to say that they had all gone to train as teachers. Sharing accommodation with them at Archer's Post meant he was able to live like a normal human being. Now he was once again no more than a fugitive.

Our trips back to the *nkang* on these late evening jaunts were invariably uneventful. I knew the Samburu enjoyed a diverse sexual life, and was surprised we never met anyone else wandering through the encampment. I was concerned for Ngalina, being widowed at such a young age and wished she had children of her own to care for her in later life. Often when a husband dies the elders appoint a part-time consort for the widow to help her bear more children in her husband's name. He will have a wife and children of his own, but the widow has no say in who is chosen. The arrangement is flexible and the consort is free to visit her as often or as infrequently as he wishes. Neither are there any financial responsibilities attached to the role, as any children resulting from this union will be looked after by the widow's family. However, no consort had ever been appointed for Ngalina and I wondered whether this was because her husband had been a Turkana or whether because in his one year of marriage the poor man had not fathered any offspring.

She was a lively and vivacious girl and I asked Lturungen whether she had any boyfriends but this, he said, was information she was unlikely to divulge to anyone. He thought that sooner or later she would be married to an elder, perhaps as his second or third wife. Certainly she could not seek the attentions of the warriors as, although they lead a promiscuous life, they are strictly forbidden to sleep with circumcised women, seeking instead the company of younger uncircumcised girls. A warrior will eventually choose one who is found to be both physically and sexually attractive. She will become his mistress and he her protector. He will present her with necklaces of beads as a token of his love until so encumbered by them she can hardly move her neck.

The arrangement is a strange one. The couple share a small dwelling of their own adjacent to her parents, but as all pervading *nkanyit* controls the relationship, she must not become pregnant, and he has to be prepared to lose her if her father decides to marry her off to an elder or a warrior nearing the end of warriorhood, as so often happens. The warriors put on a brave face and hold no grudge against the husband-to-be.

Whereas the warrior expects the girl to be faithful to him until the time of her marriage, he is not prevented from having liaisons with others to whom he can eventually turn. If he makes his partner pregnant he could find himself in real trouble, paying a fine of several cattle to the girl's father. Herbs are used to induce abortions, as is abdominal manipulation. Thereafter the girl will be circumcised and married off as quickly as possible.

Warriorhood is seen as a period when a young man can give full vent to his sexuality at a time when it matters most to him, and it prepares him well for the more sober institution of marriage which follows, and which has more to do with cementing friendships between families and building up herds of cattle than with love. The arrangement inevitably leads to older men marrying very young wives, many of whom will barely have reached puberty. Because couples from the same clan are forbidden to marry, the chances are that the bride and bridegroom of an arranged marriage will hardly be acquainted with each other. Often their marriage ceremony will be the first time they have met.

"Doesn't this sometimes lead to problems?" I asked Lpiritian. "I mean, aren't there occasions in an arranged marriage when the wife refuses to have a sexual relationship with a man who might be twice or three times her age?"

"Oh yes, but when that happens he won't force himself on her for fear of disturbing the rest of the *nkang*. That would be unseemly."

"So what happens then?"

"Well, if she continues to refuse him he will then invite all the other married couples to her house, whereupon he will copulate with her in front of them all. It doesn't matter how loudly she protests then, because everybody can see he is not being cruel to her but merely exercising his marital rights!"

Curiously the best man is also entitled to sleep with the bride when the bridegroom is away from home, unless the bridegroom expressly wishes otherwise, when the best man will be given a heifer in compensation. Even then a husband may not enjoy sole intimacy with his wife, because she is permitted to have discreet relationships with other men of his age-set.

Lturungen had experienced very little loving care in his life on account of his injury, and I think it was because of this as well as his aversion to physical closeness he found himself at variance with the sexual freedoms of his tribe. He was eternally grateful to his father for allowing him to marry a wife of his own choosing, either within or outside the tribe, and I could appreciate his determination to marry only if he could find someone in whom he could trust and to whom he could devote all his love.

CHAPTER EIGHT

Safari

head decoration for unmarried girls

"IF YOU ARE CHASED by a rhinoceros you should run a short distance, then take off your clothes and fling them high into the air in one direction while you veer off in the other. Then you drop flat on the ground. The rhino is a short-sighted animal. He will see your clothes flying through the air and will think you are still in them, so he will turn and charge after them leaving you safe on the ground where you are hiding." (I never did think to enquire what you did if you met a second rhino before you had time to put your clothes on again.)

So began lesson one of the bush highway code as interpreted by Lturungen.

"To avoid being attacked by a lion it is advisable to carry a spear, and most importantly you should wear something red."

This was lesson two of the bush code.

"That is why the *lmurran* wear red ochre in their hair and on their faces and why we favour red *nangas*. Lions fear the colour red. When they see one of us wearing red they know instinctively it could mean death."

This corresponded exactly with what I had learned from the Maasai. A lion must be very hungry indeed if it has the courage to attack our cattle when a warrior is in charge of them, I had been told. The symbiotic relationship established between the

Maasai and Samburu on the one hand and the lion on the other seemed to me just as remarkable as that of the honey guide indigenous to this area, where man and bird co-operate to mutual advantage. This small brown bird flutters around the tribesmen's heads to attract their attention, then leads them to a hive of wild bees enabling the humans to break open the hive to collect the honey, while the bird moves in to consume both the bees and the beeswax.

"One thing you can take comfort from," Lturungen continued, "is that if you are unfortunate enough to be killed by a lion it is unlikely to eat you. Only rabid lions eat human flesh."

Somehow I didn't feel this observation to be very helpful. Before leaving England I had spent a sizeable sum of money on a rabies inoculation, and in hindsight it now seemed rather a waste of money. Besides the lion, I was mindful that the dogs the Samburu kept might also carry rabies. But every Samburu dog I came across knew its place. *Nkanyit* extended even to them. They were at the bottom of the tribal hierarchy below even the livestock. They were subservient in the extreme. There was no danger of being bitten by them. You had only to say 'Hsst' in a loud voice and you would see them slink away submissively, even when meat was in the offing.

Lesson three. "If you meet a buffalo, run down the slope if there is one near you and turn a very sharp corner near a tree or a boulder. The buffalo is not able to turn very quickly because of its weight. It runs a very far distance before turning back again. Be careful too that a buffalo doesn't fool you. He may go crashing off through the undergrowth the moment you see him, and you may think you have frightened him away, but the chances are he has turned around and is lying in wait watching you from the cover of bushes and ready to charge you the moment your attention wanders."

Of the 'big five' I encountered only elephant when we were out on safari. The buffalo had succumbed to the drought of 1984 in great quantities, and their numbers were still depleted. Those which remained preferred to keep close to the river banks. Although there were lion around they, together with the rhinoceros, had suffered dreadfully at the hands of the trigger-happy Shifta rather than through natural causes, and because of the drought the few which remained had made for the Shaba and Samburu National Reserves where they knew instinctively they were assured of water. We saw merely a solitary cheetah.

Now it is the Somali Shifta who are the greatest threat to life. The Samburu, who prize spears above all other weapons, are effective against these bandits, picking them off singly out in the open. These acts of bravery are recognised by the elders who award copper bracelets to the warriors as an indication of valour. Formerly they would have been in recognition of killing a lion single-handed. One particularly tough-looking young gentleman I came across boasted several such bracelets on his arm. Nevertheless a spear is less effective when a *nkang* full of defenceless women and children comes under attack. So the government has set up a Samburu 'Home Guard', one man with a rifle being assigned to every three or four encampments.

Before I visited East Africa I imagined each species of animal would occupy a special habitat all of its own, separated from the others by hills or rivers or forests in much the same way that they are segregated by cages in a zoo. It came as a great surprise to find them all spread out on the plains in view of each other as if they were in one gigantic field. I could look around and see lion here, wildebeest there, a sprinkling of antelope in this place and zebra in that, and a leopard surveying them all from the branches of a lone tree. Protected in groups, the herbivores keep a wary eye on their predators. There is safety in numbers, but woe betide any who become separated or who are left behind when the herd is on the run. Their days — indeed their hours — are numbered. When the offspring of most animals are born they remain at their place of birth for days or even weeks until they are strong enough to accompany the adults. Not so the young of the wildebeest and the antelope, who within minutes of birth are up on their legs following the herd. Without this ability they would never survive their predators.

Any other part of the globe must be hard-pressed to surpass Kenya's range and variety of animals and birds. And seldom are species more varied than in the primeval wilderness of Samburuland, where there is a giraffe with one tufted horn between its ears instead of the usual two. A zebra with such thin black and white stripes that it looks like the forerunner of the bar code. The gerenuk, an animal with the body of an antelope and a neck borrowed from a giraffe. The Besia oryx, which has fooled generations into thinking it was the mythical unicorn, and the blue-knickered Somali ostrich.

The absence of the bigger animals in no way detracted from the pleasure of watching the wildlife. It was marvellous to be out on the plains with these creatures, observing them from the ground instead of from the relative isolation of a safari vehicle where at best one can achieve only a passing acquaintance. As time passed, so I began to learn something of the character and temperament of each of them.

The dimensions of the giraffe seemed to be entirely out of proportion to their surroundings. For all their size they have a gracefulness in both body and movement which, when they browse on the tree tops, gives them the appearance of floating over the surface of the plains like a ship sailing before a breeze. And when they gallop, those long and sinuous legs, which move in unison on each flank like the camel, give the animal the appearance of rolling from side to side like a boat in a choppy sea. The reticulated giraffe, which is peculiar to this area, has a deep liver-red-coloured skin marked with a coarse network of fine white lines. It seemed to me incongruous that a beast with such delicate features should live all its life off an indigestible diet of leaves and twigs from the thorny acacias, their long black tongues covering the sturdy spines in a viscous saliva in preparation for a precipitous descent to the stomach. Although giraffe drink occasionally when water is available, bending low with splayed legs, their diet makes them virtually impervious to drought.

Wherever we went we saw small groups of Grevy's zebra, an

animal so far removed from other species of zebra that it cannot interbreed. Bigger, with prominent round ears like table tennis bats, it has narrow stripes falling into a chevron pattern on its fore- and hindquarters which make it look as though it is wearing striped tights several sizes too big for it. The Swahili name for zebra is 'striped donkey', and that is just about what they are. The various breeds are comely looking animals, and at first glance look appealing with their chubby cheeks and curvaceous backsides slashed with such gaudy markings. However, on longer acquaintance the appeal wears thin.

I suppose from their zany looks I imagined them to be the clowns of the animal kingdom, but I soon established that playful humour was not part of their makeup. When you first approach them they are inquisitive and feign good behaviour, but when the novelty of human surveillance wears off you see them in their true colours, the hoi polloi of the plains, gaudy, vulgar, ill-mannered and sour-tempered and, like donkeys, they can deliver a vicious kick. You have only to see a couple of males fighting to appreciate that they have never been acquainted with the Queensberry Rules.

In contrast I never tired of watching the graceful and shy antelope, like the toy-like dik dik. Standing no more than fourteen inches high, these strongly territorial animals mark out the boundaries of their domain with a tar-like substance which exudes from the glands on either side of their face. You always find them in pairs, and they mate for life. Curiously enough they have a trait shared with the rhinoceros, in that both animals leave their dung in one place. Over a period of time it becomes quite a mound. When it comes to competitiveness, that created by the rhinoceros is always the clear winner!

The gerenuk — the long-necked antelope — lives entirely off the leaves of the acacias. It seems to obtain all its moisture from this source and never needs to drink. I would see them standing daintily on their hind legs, their forelegs resting on branches and their slender bodies and long necks stretched as high as they could to reach the more succulent morsels, their agile mouths carefully avoiding the thorns. The animal quite changes in character when it runs, shrinking in stature as it hunches its neck to its body in a manner, I suppose, designed to avoid colliding with low-hanging branches.

It was a joy to see Lpiritian track down some of these creatures. He would signal to me to follow him so that we could creep up in a way which made them unaware of our presence. I loved to see their heads looking out inquisitively through the camouflage of foliage, two bright beady eyes and a button nose, their neck and long oval ears giving their heads the symmetry of a three-bladed propeller. When at times branches obscured the larger part of their flanks and long necks, their heads seemed disembodied, floating dreamily among the leaves, and I fancied them as the spirits of the woodland.

It saddened me that Lturungen could not join us in these escapades. In spite of his foot he would at times cover the ground much faster than I could, but he always needed to concentrate on where he was stepping which made it difficult for him to follow animals, and crouching was in any case very painful for him.

Once or twice we caught sight of the Besia oryx with their handsome heads of dark and light markings and rapier-like horns which, when seen sideways, could be mistaken for the single horn of the unicorn. Lpiritian admired these animals not only because of their good looks but also because they are one of the few capable of seeing off lion.

Flocks of the vulturine guinea fowl, with their startling blue breast feathers, crossed and recrossed our path and yellow-necked spur fowls and ground squirrels were everywhere. When we scrambled up the rocky outcrops we often scattered the hyraxes, small brownish-grey animals about the size of a beaver which emit a high-pitched shriek in alarm. I would never have believed they are the nearest relative to the elephant and share many of their characteristics, including a ridiculously long gestation period for such small animals of about seven months. I wondered how on earth they could run up the near-vertical rock faces around us, until Lpiritian explained they have a kind of rubber pad on their feet which sweats when they run so that they can go up the smooth surfaces. Without doubt the bigger creatures are impressive, but for me these little ones were full of interest.

Above us, and hanging conspicuously almost in celebration, were the brown fruits of the sausage trees (*Kigelia africana*) looking for all the world like continental sausages, while the acacias were festooned with the pendulous cone-shaped nests of weaver birds whose incessant chatter was the muzak of the plains. At our feet the industrious dung beetles were busy propelling little balls of dung they had collected in which they would lay their eggs. And rising sharply out of the plains like outsize children's sand-castles were red and orange termite mounds, the grains of sandy soil glued together so effectively by the insects' secretions that you could easily climb them to gain an elevated view of the land around.

In the woodland there were gaudy Superb starlings, orange on the under side, blue and green on the wings and back, a dark head, bright eyes and a white undertail. There were many hornbills with their distinctive curved and oversized beaks. I was ill at ease at the way the Samburu treated their women, yet by any standards the behaviour of the male hornbill is bizarre. After mating he actually imprisons the female in her nesting hole in a tree by plastering up the entrance, and doesn't release her again until the young are hatched, feeding both her and her young through a tiny slit in the prison wall.

It seemed that the Samburu will always go out of their way to avoid conflict with the larger animals and, unless surprised at close quarters, most animals will keep well clear of humans. Conflict, when it comes, invariably revolves around lions, hyenas and jackals or other predators attacking Samburu livestock, or elephants blundering into their encampments.

All animals are treated with respect. In the days before the game laws and with only the spear or bow and arrow as their main hunting weapon, there appeared to have been very little wanton killing, in stark contrast to the attitude of the Europeans who killed merely for the fun of it and for self-aggrandizement.

Throughout Africa the native herders, hunters and farmers have always cared for the land and its animals. In African tradition the land and its creatures are inhabited by a spirit and a descending chain of lesser spirits. For the Samburu and Maasai that spirit is Nkai, the one who provides for every need. They believe the land does not belong to them, but it is their heritage. It has not been provided to serve the needs of just this generation or the next. It is there for all generations for as long as man lives on earth. That is why they do not fence it off, put up boundaries or sell it in parcels. Were we to share the same attitude we would think carefully before exploiting the earth for commercial gain. We would pay far more attention to organic farming, to the disposal of waste materials and to mining and quarrying.

Likewise, animals are killed only when the need arises so that their stocks are preserved for posterity, in the same way that their forebears handed them down to the present generation. The native tribes of Africa were the true conservationists, as are most undeveloped peoples. Only because of the greed and the despoliation of modern man is it necessary to set up parks and reserves to reinstate harmony with nature. The current conflict between the nomads and their governments, anxious to pin them down into settled communities so that they can be taxed and controlled and their lands sold off, is far greater than any conflict between man and animal.

Relying almost entirely on their herds for food, the Samburu have never eaten birds, eggs, fish or carnivores although in times of drought and when journeying through the bush they used to hunt ungulates like oryx and gazelle to supplement their food supply and to conserve their herds. Neither would they hunt elephant, believing it to be too human in character to be eaten.

Since the introduction of game laws the Samburu have been

obliged to increase their herds of goat as a standby in place of gazelle. It is an indication of the adaptability of the tribe that before these laws were introduced and at a time before poaching and indiscriminate hunting decimated the animals, the Samburu used the tough rhinoceros hide for sandals, making them fleet of foot in their harsh terrain, and giving them superiority over neighbouring tribes in times of attack and during cattle raids. Giraffe skin was used for buckets and water containers. Married women's necklaces (*mporro*) were made from the hair of giraffes' tails and rings of ivory were invariably used to decorate the earlobes of warriors.

Now the Samburu, in common with most other nomads, wear sandals fashioned from old rubber tyres, and tins and plastic containers have taken the place of buckets. The women have turned from giraffes' tails and have started to use the fibres from palm leaves for their necklaces, and ivory earplugs (*lkiyaa loltomia*) are carefully handed down from one warrior age-set to another. This adaptability has been going on for many generations, and is likely to have been the norm for centuries. Certainly skins were worn before the advent of cloth, and personal ornaments were made from wood, ivory, shells and leather before beads were introduced into Kenya by the slave traders. Given this ability to change and to modify, the Samburu lifestyle is likely to survive for a long time still, unless future governments forcibly take their lands away from them.

Often when we went on longer safaris the boys would take maize flour and fat with them in brown paper packets, and in the heat of the day we would shelter under the shade of trees and cook *posho*. This was a blessed relief for Lturungen, for being in the company of men and well away from the presence of women he could eat to his heart's content. Sometimes we cheated and lit a fire with matches. On other occasions, however, we used the age-old method of rubbing two sticks together. The pattern of rubbing a pointed wooden spindle between one's palms, the point being lodged in a notched piece of wood laid along the ground is one which is used in many parts of the world. Only the kindling is different. In this instance either elephant or donkey dung is used, both being readily combustible when dried in the sun.

It didn't take long to cook the *posho* and we would eat straight from the pot, scooping up the white glutinous mass with our hands and washing it down with water, the boys often drinking from water-holes which looked far from clean, while I used some sterilised water I carried with me. I found this food remarkably satisfying. It surprised me because I would not have looked at it twice if I had been given it at home. Somehow one's taste for food seems to change on visits to other lands. At home I am addicted to strong, unsweetened tea, cake, sticky buns and vegetables. And yet when we visit the other half of the family in Norway nothing seems more natural than a hot cup of strong black coffee and a slice of cheese on flatbread. Staying with friends in Czech Republic, a country which seems to know no other vegetable except the ubiquitous gherkin, the inevitable pork and dumplings goes down a treat.

And so it was here; never once did the thought of vegetables or buns cross my mind. I enjoyed the sweet weak tea we were served in the morning, and the litre of thick cow's or camel's milk mixed with a little blood which followed it filled the stomach remarkably effectively. The milk itself had a strong smoky flavour given to it by the gourd it was stored in. When they are empty these gourds are sterilised with sticks from a tree the Samburu called *serechoi*. These sticks are first burnt in the fire and whilst still flaming are thrust into the gourd. The flame is extinguished through the lack of oxygen and the gourd fills with smoke. The same process is repeated four or five times, and then the gourd is ready to be replenished with milk. The smoke contains a preserving agent which prevents the milk from turning sour for up to three days in temperatures which out of doors reach 41° centigrade.

About a litre of blood is taken from each of the cattle once a month. It is an important source of nutrition for the tribe while at the same time preserving the size of the herd. A rope is put round the neck of the animal and pulled tight so that it partially loses consciousness, but is still able to stand. The rope also causes the jugular vein to protrude. A flanged arrow is shot at the vein piercing it just deep enough for the blood to flow. The blood is collected in a tin or a gourd and as soon as it is full the rope is released. The bleeding stops immediately. The animal regains full consciousness and it slapped on its rump and sent on its way. The container of blood is then stirred vigorously with a stick for five or so minutes. This separates out the coagulant which appears as a red slimy mass round the length of the stick when it is withdrawn. The stick is then thrown to the dogs who consume the coagulant with relish.

The blood, while remaining bright red, is nevertheless thin and watery and has none of the flavour one usually associates with it. At special ceremonies the blood is drunk neat, but normally it is kept to be mixed with milk. If I had not seen it being added I would never have known that I drank milk which contained blood. The smokiness overpowered all other flavours, and the milk itself was thick enough to absorb the red of the oxyhaemoglobin.

Sometimes when we went on safari there were only the three of us — Lpiritian, Lturungen and myself — but often one or more half brothers and some of the warriors accompanied us as well. There was a great sense of camaraderie on these occasions, and I enjoyed immensely the company of these young people. Lpiritian, with perhaps his half brother Senene, were the quietest of the group. Nevertheless Lpiritian was enjoying his month-long holiday from the tourist lodge, and had rediscovered his zest for life. The warriors were full of fun and sociable good humour, and engaged in plenty of playful teasing and leg-pulling.

Among their numbers were Longoloto and his companion, the serious-minded Jonathan, brother of Nasaba, Buni's wife. Both these boys were later to become guardians for Karaito and Lobuka once they had joined the warrior age-set. Lturungen too enjoyed the freedom of these expeditions, although there were days when the walking made his foot raw, limiting the distance he could travel.

At first the little group did not know how to treat me. Lpiritian and Lturungen believed that a man of my age would tire quickly in the intense heat. They knew nothing of the qualities of mad dogs and Englishmen. They felt responsible for my welfare and on the first of the longer treks, and without prior reference to me, manufactured an armchair out of sticks and branches and *nangas* in which I could rest while they prepared *posho*. Their care and attention was very touching. They failed to realise how slowly an African walks in comparison with the average European. Although our trek had taken a long time in burning sun, I was far from tired. I sat in the chair in recognition of their kindness, but it did my morale no good for it made me believe they regarded me as an old man.

It wasn't long before the boys came to realise I could keep up with them, and that I did not find sitting or lying on the ground out in the wilds in the least bit demeaning. Eventually they came to regard me no differently from the rest of their number, and in my own perception I slipped gratefully from the level of a senior to a junior elder.

Those days spent out on the plains were golden. The sense of freedom was immense. The vistas were breathtaking, the scattered mountains rose sheer out of the stony ground like enormous fortresses shimmering in the heat. The vision was stark and awesome. The emptiness, wildness and utter isolation assumed qualities I had not experienced before. This was the Africa of my dreams, dreams which had been with me since I was a child. Palm-fringed coastlines and blinding white sands were alluring, but similar beaches could be found in other places in the world. The little green hills of western Kenya with their trees and small fields and small round thatched huts were endearing, but no more typified the Africa of boyhood imagination than the prairie-like Athi plain or the rolling hills and grasslands of the Maasai Mara. No, it was the savage beauty of the land north of the Wuaso Ngiro which embodied my Africa, the Africa of adventure and exploration.

I remembered myself dressed in cub uniform walking along suburban streets in the warmth of a midsummer evening, the heat still reflecting from the pavements — the burning tropical sun. Our task was to track down and collect pieces of coloured wool which had been tied to hedges, railings and gate posts — the spoor of elephant and rhinoceros with the skyline searched for hostile natives. Now, some forty-five years later, here I was in that self-same land, not as a serving officer of the British Empire nor as part of a sanitised safari package, but on my own and in the company of those very natives I had imagined to be hostile.

Only after the magic of a thunderstorm does the dry open thorn bush country through which we travelled suddenly burst into spring-like green. Then, the acacias bloom in all their creamy-yellow finery. Now the pent-up energy still lay expectant in every twig and branch and stem awaiting the trigger of rain to unleash the miracle of new life and growth, rain which seemed as if it would never come.

The sky was filled with high grey clouds, too high to give more than a passing shower even though the boys continued to look longingly to the horizon for the thunderclouds they had so long awaited. The soil was darkened where the rain had fallen and the dust no longer flew up at our feet. Already little green wisps of grass had sprouted out of the ground, and on the thorn bushes leaf buds had swelled, glistening and sticky to the touch, waiting and hoping for the rain which would cause them to burst out into new green foliage. These poor barren plants showed so much patience in their privation and such willingness to burst forth with natural beauty that I felt providence could not withhold the rain much longer.

Lturungen was quick to notice my wonder at the change brought about by this little shower. He explained it did, as I had imagined, take only a single heavy thunderstorm to transform the look of the plains. The leaves and flowers would burst out of the branches almost while you stood and looked at them. Sometimes the rain came so suddenly and with such force that a mighty wall of water several feet high rushed down the previously dry watercourses. Then it could be perilous, and animals and people were swept away and drowned as had happened to one of his brothers.

The desert was not devoid of people. Encampments were to be found wherever there was reasonable grazing. Sometimes we would pass two or three young children sitting in the shade of trees as they tended their goats, or perhaps older children in charge of cattle. We would pass women with enormous loads of firewood on their backs and warriors on safari in their twos and threes. No one passed without engaging in conversation. Inevitably questions were asked as to where one was travelling to and from, and snippets of news and gossip were exchanged at the same time. It was the Samburu grapevine in action. By this means news travelled astonishingly quickly throughout the tribal network, and served to create unity and cohesion amongst the eight clans of the 'Loikop'.

Women usually engaged in conversation from a distance. The forms of greeting are numerous, depending upon the sex and order of seniority within the tribe, but the warriors came up and shook hands with me exchanging greetings with the word *Supa!* No one expressed the slightest surprise at seeing a *mzungu* travelling across the plain. They assumed I did not speak their language and never tried to strike up a conversation. Only if I used some Samburu words or place names in conversation with Lpiritian or Lturungen did they express astonishment, as if I were breaking into their private world.

It is the abruptness of the mountains which, as they rise out of the ground about them, gives the plains the appearance of being flat. Yet the appearance is illusory, for the land rises and falls like the waves after a storm. These gentle undulations added interest and excitement to our travels, for as the crest of each low ridge was reached so a new vista was revealed and the distant mountains appeared ever more stark on the horizon.

This is an eroded landscape. The mountains are formed of harder, impervious rock which has left them standing high and dry above the surrounding desert. They formed an outer boundary to our field of vision and gave us a feeling of security and seclusion as we went on our way. Each had its own unmistakeable character, and by observing them across the open empty desert you could use them as navigational aids wherever you travelled on the plains.

Here was one with lots of little peaks, each peak looking as though it was holding hands with its neighbour, and here was a long low one so tired of watching the passage of time in this ageless landscape that it had lain down and gone to sleep. There was a conspicuous one over there which looked like the rear view of a hypacrosaurus resting on the ground, his tail buried in the plains, his dorsal crest dominating the mountain ridge.

To the north was a ridiculous pair of mountains, or were they more like gigantic slabs of rock? One crouched on the ground in the form of a frightened mouse, while the other rose above it like a cat about to pounce. Not unnaturally the employees of the safari lodges nicknamed these two the Cat and Mouse, but in reality I am sure the notion was put into their heads by a misinterpretation of 'Nkadori Multo', the Samburu name for them which has nothing to do with animals but means 'tall necks'. To the east of the Cat and Mouse were two or three long low humps which looked like sleeping elephants, and all around us, closer than the mountains, were joyful little hills rising playfully from the desert floor.

There was one central feature standing in splendid isolation which I have yet to describe, and to which both the surrounding mountains and the tribesmen paid homage, and that was the great bulk of Ol doinyo Sabachi. You could not help but wonder at it. It stood there, surrounded by desert — magnificent, all-seeing and silent — the sphinx of Samburuland. This table mountain with its broad flat summit has a southern face of sheer granitoid gneiss, which tops a breathtaking height of 6,000ft. Rising so high above the plains it has its own micro-climate, and woodland covers its lower slopes and crowns its plateau.

On one occasion we climbed Sabachi, beginning at dawn to avoid the heat of the day. Our route lay along the gradual slopes of its eastern flank beginning in acacia woodland and then rising through vegetation which became green and dense. We walked warily. There were leopard about and the boys were convinced we would encounter one. They need not have worried. Leopards are shy animals and the noise made by our party would surely have frightened them away.

After an hour of walking in crisp clear air with the rising sun pleasantly warm on our backs, we reached a saddle and were greeted by a spectacular view of the Matthews Range, hazy blue in the early light. The path beyond was clearly marked but steep. It took nearly another hour before we came to a small plateau where we rested. An enormous tree high on the skyline marked the summit. Its presence gave us encouragement for the final steep ascent. Our climb ended abruptly as we reached the top of the escarpment. Once on the table top our route ran across pavements of rock interspersed with rich pasture, marsh and lush woodland. In contrast to the plains, there is bird song and butterflies in abundance. The meadows are attractive to the Samburu in times of drought and there were a number of young boys herding cattle. They lived on the mountain by themselves and would be separated from their families in the plains for weeks at a time. Caring for cattle in such isolation is a considerable responsibility for eleven and twelve year olds and plays an important part in the development of self-confidence, independence and integrity so characteristic of Samburu males.

We stopped at one of their encampments. The shelters they lived in were different from any I had seen before — shaped like tents with a ridge pole and sloping sides constructed from sticks and brushwood covered with mud and dung. No one was about, but as is the Samburu custom, we helped ourselves to milk from the gourds lying around.

The view from the southern face was stunning — southward

across to Archer's Post the Wuaso Ngiro and the high ground beyond, westward to the Kalama mountains, and eastward to the rim of the plains as they sink to the Lorian Swamp. Nowhere was the hand of man evident to the naked eye save for the pencil like line of the road north to Marsabit and the Ethiopian border. The expanse was so vast it was as if we had the world at our feet. We stood in awed silence. Now I understood why the Samburu came here to be near Nkai.

I came to realise that it is the juxtaposition of the vertical with the horizontal which makes this landscape so exhilarating. Often as we journeyed, the crest of the ridge would obscure the plains which lay beyond, cutting across the horizon in a clear hard line like the edge of the sea as it meets the sky, yet the mountains could not be obscured. Their bulk still rose majestically above the ridge, sharp against the radiant firmament, those towering vertical masses punctuating the crest in their ones and twos, some close at hand, others far off, in a way which enhanced the spatial dimension. The revelation of height, breadth and distance in these situations was sensational, and the intensity of light in the unpolluted air heightened the visual impact.

On fine mornings when the sun rose in a clear sky, Sabachi would hide away in mist as if the brilliance of the dawn was too great for its granitoid face to contemplate. As the morning wore on, so the haze lifted to leave a circlet of little white clouds atop its peak. When its adversary, the sun, was itself obscured by cloud, then Sabachi would emerge boldly from the haze to look down on the surrounding plain, its darkened form defiant, its challenge inescapable. I liked it best in the late afternoon when the sun shone like a fiery disc, its white light transmuted to molten gold. Then the lowering rays would strike the red and orange of soil and rock and Sabachi would glow with an intensity as if it were aflame, while the distant peaks of other mountains trembled in the liquid light.

It was at this time of day the desert was at its best. The dying heat of the sun was rejoined by reflected heat from the earth, and in the ensuing equilibrium the breeze died for a while and the land fell into a hushed stillness. The blaze of light in the west cast long shadows over the ground, enhancing the perspective and distorting concepts of distance and space. It was on just such an afternoon in the silence of a dying day that I fell into a state of contemplation.

At my feet was a termite mound which rose to shoulder height, and on top of which I had made Lturungen stand while I photographed him facing the sun as it dropped towards the Kalama mountains of his birth. As I looked at the mound I thought of the hundreds of industrious insects which had formed this pile, a city as busy as any I had known, just one of thousands dotted across the desert floor. I imagined each of those creatures commanded by the irresistible force of instinct, driven by the urge to build, blindly following the demands of the colony, their energy sapped by the dictates of their own little world. I wondered at their organisation, their devotion to duty, their discipline, a multitude of scurrying bodies each bent upon fulfilling its allotted task. Was there not a single individual among them? Would not just one of them turn aside to contemplate the wide world which lay beyond its nest? Were they to transcend their obsession with the soil and to gaze upon the lofty heights of far-off mountains, they would have seen how puny were their labours, how minuscule the pinnacle of their aspirations.

My eyes turned from the mound to the setting sun and the distant peaks, the lengthening shadows adding ever more to the distances separating them from myself. And as I raised my eyes I was conscious that here was I, a mere human being, able to take in the world of the termite at a glance and yet no less inspired by the grandeur and sweep of the landscape, and the glowing orb in the sky. How difficult it is to grapple with concepts of space and size and infinity! In my cognition these mountains were huge, their weight and volume unimaginable, yet how infinitely greater was the sun as it now dipped to meet them, hanging like a pendant above the mantle of the earth, and was not this gargantuan furnace but a speck within the boundless universe? And did not infinity lie beyond even that?

And while I followed the course of the sun as it descended behind the mountains I was aware of accusing fingers, the fingers of every shadow pointing at me, and I felt so terribly small and insignificant in the immensity of creation. A great cry of anguish rent my heart. Could I ever again forsake contemplation of the eternal for the tawdry pleasures of a mundane temporal life?

The dying sun consumed the sky in its radiance, and heaven and earth were caught up in a song of light. My anguish turned to ecstasy; joy at being alive, joy at witnessing the majesty of creation, a joy which tugged at my heart, gave full measure, knew no bounds.

"You are a part of this," it said. "All this is man's heritage. Do not question, do not doubt, do not measure or define. It is a gift from divinity. Accept and be glad!"

Then the sun set, and above the darkened outline of the mountains the sky flushed with soft, rosy colours of the afterglow and a handful of birds called to me as they flew home to roost. The plains faded into soft greys and fawns. Darkness fell, and a breeze arose from the desert, stirring the branches of the acacias until they found repose in a breathless starry night.

CHAPTER NINE

Living the Samburu Way

the Njilii

"WHERE ARE the leaves?" I asked Lturungen.

"What leaves?" came the reply.

I distinctly remembered Lturungen saying to the schoolchildren "For toilets we use bushes, and for toilet paper we use leaves."

We had been to see the cattle watered, had washed ourselves, returned to the *lorora* to drink milk and were now lying in the shade of trees in a nearby *lbaan*. I was just about to set out to find a convenient bush when I realised there was not a single leaf of a suitable size anywhere to be seen.

When I explained what leaves I meant, Lturungen looked uncomfortable.

"It's the drought, you see, there are no suitable leaves left."

"Then what do you use?"

"Well, you see these stones ..." He pointed to the sandy soil which was liberally strewn with golf ball-sized quartz pebbles ribbed with red and orange veins. "We use these."

I stared at them for a moment. Hard and unrelenting round pebbles. The quartz sparkled back at me cheerfully as the rays of the sun glanced off their smooth surfaces. There were hundreds of them — no, thousands! They lay everywhere you looked. This was a totally new concept in personal hygiene. I thought of an advert frequently seen on television. I imagined the reaction of shoppers confronted by a pile of pebbles in the supermarket at home in place of the familiar rolls of toilet paper. The supply of these stones would outlast any roll of toilet paper, no matter what its length, but what about those other qualities — qualities of softness and absorbency? I suppose stones could be classed as a 'green product' for they are certainly environmentally friendly, but I was not so sure about absorbency. The situation was absurd.

I got up and wandered off, collecting pebbles as I went. The ground was searingly hot beyond the shade of the trees, and the pebbles were hot to touch. I found a bush suitably distant from our little company. I squatted down. With only a single piece of cloth wrapped around me, that side of it was delightfully easy. Then the time came to use the pebbles. They were hot enough to the hand, but when I came to apply them to a particularly delicate part of the anatomy, I let out a cry of pain. For one moment I thought I had been cauterised. There was no need to worry about their quality of absorbency — any moisture evaporated immediately.

Back at the *lbaan* the boys enquired whether I had managed all right. I explained why I had found the episode such a painful experience, and they rolled around on the ground in agonised laughter.

"We should have remembered to warn you to take the pebbles from where they lie in the shade. Either that, or you use a bush only in the morning or the evening."

In the climate of Samburuland's plains, babies and young children wander around naked and so there is never any need of nappies, and if a child messes on its mother she counts it a blessing. Neither are the men discreet when on their own and away from the company of women. It was not unusual for them to urinate in the middle of a conversation with you.

Samburu family and social life is centred on the *nkang*. It is here the elders live with their wives and children, and it is where they entertain their guests. Goats, sheep, the women's donkeys, and cows and camels kept for milking or too young to go with the rest of the herd, are also based on the *nkang*. The rest of the cattle and camels are in the care of the older boys and warriors who live away from the village in temporary stockades while they move from pasture to pasture.

It is the elders who decide on the site of the *nkang* and when it should move to a new location. The villages are often tucked away on the edge of a watercourse or on a slightly elevated piece of land out in the open. The availability of grazing is the prime reason for moving home rather than water. You can, after all, carry water to your home, but you can't very well transport grazing. Each *nkang* is shared by two or more close families living within the circular confines of the thorn hedge. Lpiritian's *nkang* was occupied by just his family and one other. They had been in that spot for several months, and were contemplating moving again to find better grazing for the goats.

Samburuland is not uniformly arid. Some parts, especially the areas in the larger mountain ranges, are well watered and the vegetation relatively lush, the tallest peaks carrying a mantle of thick refreshing forest and undergrowth. Yet Lpiritian's family had always lived in the sunsoaked plains, preferring the arid semi-desert even though grass was sparse because the cattle survived better there in times of drought on account of the abundance of minerals and salts in the soil.

The elders moved the *nkang* a number of times each year. Other villages moved with similar frequency. Families were therefore continually circulating, and by so doing they maintained a wide mesh of acquaintances and an extensive web of friends to call upon in times of need. In a world where the majority of mankind has permanent dwellings, the consequences of an itinerant life are sometimes difficult to grasp. I remembered schoolchildren in England being shocked when Lturungen explained to them he had no idea where home would be when he returned to Kenya, and would have to go looking in the plains and enquire of people he knew before he could locate his family.

These people wander as free as a dream. They are less tied even than the gypsies since they have no caravans to pull around and no roads to follow. Although the longer sticks and poles are transported from place to place on the backs of donkeys, the *ngajii* itself is never built twice in exactly the same way. New hearthstones will be used each time, and if there is not a ready supply of cow dung with which to plaster the roof because of the animals being kept away on distant grazing lands, then skins, woven fibres or even flattened tin cans will be put to use. Personal belongings are negligible, no one owning more than can be transported on the back of a donkey and their wealth, namely their livestock, walks with them on four legs.

With no ties of property, land, money or belongings and none of the disciplines of employment, these people are truly free — being free in mind and free in spirit enhances the stature of each individual, enabling them to devote all their energies to just living and being. It is true that drought, death and hardship are never far away but that aside, day follows glorious day and the tribe lets life unfold before it, accepting what comes its way with an unequivocal and almost saintly indifference. There is no striving, no anguish, little jealousy and relatively few worries.

The degree of liberty which a nomad enjoys, the effect of having the limitless earth to wander over yet with none of the responsibilities of ploughing and sowing, is a liberty almost unimaginable to an urban dweller. Is there still a last vestige of our earlier days within some of us — some half-forgotten desire which has not been put to rest, and which we seek to satisfy through being outdoors, walking, riding, cycling, or even motoring in the countryside? And are there not two kinds of gardeners — those who dig and hoe and sow and are primarily cultivators at heart — and those content to own merely an expanse of grass and trees around their homes, not to cultivate but to provide them with some semblance of the freedom enjoyed by our ancestors; land on which to wander freely, no matter how small an area it may be?

Life in the *nkang* is well ordered and men, women and children each have their allotted tasks. The men construct the thorn hedge, the corrals for the animals and when necessary, dig wells. They also decide, according to custom, the location of each family within the *nkang*. However the *ngajii* is the domain of the woman. It is her house and hers alone. She builds it and maintains it, and she allows her husband and his friends to share it. Each house is positioned within the *nkang* in hierarchical order, the wife of the senior elder being first followed clockwise by his other wives in order of seniority, the wives of the other elders and then the widows in the order in which they married their husbands. The women are amazingly quick at building their homes, often accomplishing the task in a few hours so that even when the family moves to a new location it will not be without a roof over its head at night. Only women are permitted to build houses which explains why Lturungen, being unmarried, had no home of his own. Each hut has its own gateway through the thorn hedge and although the men build the stockade, it is the women who decide where the gates will be.

Almost all the household chores are done by the women, helped with the cheery assistance of the younger children. The goats are small enough for these youngsters to handle themselves. They treat them lovingly, one holding a nanny while the other does the milking from the right-hand teats, those on the left being reserved for the kids. Although I often stood and watched I was never allowed to lend a hand as milking was a task strictly reserved for women and children. When their mothers struggled under loads of firewood heaped on their backs, the children valiantly carried all they could under their arms, and while food was being cooked the children occupied themselves sterilising the empty milk gourds with burning sticks. The women draw water for domestic use, and they make all kinds of utensils using a primitive chisel to hollow out both gourds and wood from which they manufacture containers for milk, yoghurt, sugar, tea and other household items. They also make bead necklaces, weave mats from fibres, prepare medicines and snuff, and help with the birth of young animals. Yet they still have plenty of time each day to sit and chat with their friends and neighbours and to play with the young children.

I longed to be able to talk to the women to find out more about the world they occupied — a world so separate from that of their menfolk — but it was to remain veiled from me. None of them understood English, but more significantly, in the same way that husband and wife expressed no emotional attachment to each other in public, so also they never discussed anything of a personal nature, all such matters being shared only with others of the same sex. Lpiritian simply refused to indulge in conversation with Morissa on my behalf, and so the lives of the women in the *nkang* remained an enigma.

This extraordinary reticence between sexes is not confined to the Samburu. The young Pokot tribesman who stayed with us in England some years earlier told me the highlight of his stay was his freedom to talk to girls. Young Lokwang and our eldest daughter sat for hours wrapped in conversation, and he was genuinely surprised to find that women had ideas, ideals and opinions of their own. It was as if he were exploring a whole new concept of human relations. Lturungen, too, delighted in the same experience and particularly enjoyed the freedom which his Kenyan school had given him to study alongside girls from other tribes who had a more liberal view of the capabilities and interests of their womenfolk than his nomadic society had.

The segregation of men and women was an aspect of Samburu life Lturungen found abhorrent, and upon which he commented frequently.

Yet it was him to whom I turned to answer some of the questions I would have asked of Morissa. Whereas he himself maintained he would never marry more than one wife, he nevertheless believed polygamy had its advantages, especially for those living in such harsh conditions as the Samburu.

"Almost invariably the first wife welcomes the arrival of

others," he affirmed. "After all, she has more companionship and additional help with the daily round of chores. Yet as the first wife she still retains her position of seniority. Nor are the wives treated as they would be in a harem — each has their own *ngajii*, and the husband normally lives with each of them in turn. As a consequence, babies are well spaced. Also children are not weaned until they are nearly three years old, and so wives are spared the strain of frequent births. Besides, the more wives a man has the more they can exercise control over him, often to their advantage rather than his."

I could see polygamy had other advantages too, especially for the children. The family circle is large and children have a degree of security they would be unlikely to enjoy in other societies. A child could go to any of the mothers when it wanted food or drink or comfort. The diverse characteristics and abilities contributed by the wives to the larger family meant that each child experienced a broad upbringing, and in turn developed a more rounded personality. Moreover, if one of the wives died there was the safeguard of other mothers to nurture her offspring. Married siblings welcomed the youngest ones into their own homes. Those who were yet to marry encouraged the youngsters to play and contributed to their development and learning, and in so doing were themselves being trained in parental responsibilities against the time when they married and had children of their own. It seemed to me that the youngsters of a large family enjoyed a sort of permanent party atmosphere.

Some outsiders would maintain that this type of communal family living within the rigid framework of tribal rules suppresses individualism and hinders its members in developing their full potential. Yet for the nomad survival is uppermost. Individualism is therefore a luxury which cannot be afforded when each has to row together with the others for the good of all. Even if it were affordable, would it be of any real benefit? The tribe adapts of its own volition in the face of changing circumstances. Did it really need individual thought and expression to help it develop in a new direction and to seek higher aspirations, when its people appeared so content with their lifestyle and lived in harmony with the land? The security afforded the individual by both the family unit and tribal discipline engenders confidence. And confidence is the best climate in which to nurture personality. For me it was the flowering of these individual personalities which made living with the Samburu such a delight.

Although discipline is pervasive, the tribe applies it sensitively and imaginatively. Tensions between teenager and parent are carefully avoided. During the critical years of warriorhood the education, training and discipline of these young men is the prerogative of the firestick elders who are always two age-sets senior to them. Since there must always be two age-sets between those of father and son, fathers have no responsibility for their teenage offspring. Instead it is the firestick elders who guide them through these difficult years and who ensure they accord respect to their parents. Similarly most girls are wedded before the onset of teenage years and grow to maturity in the company of their husband's family rather than their own.

I never called Morissa by her name. It would have been improper to do so. A name is considered too intimate a possession to be used on a day-to-day basis even when one has been to school and is given a Christian name. I recalled the unease felt by our Luyha friends when at first we referred to them by their Christian names rather than as the Mother and Father of their firstborn. Even Lpiritian referred to his wife as *mparatut* (wife), and in return she used the word *lpayian* (husband). I did, however, use the prerogative of being a European to call Lpiritian and Lturungen by their forenames. Morissa referred to Nasaba as *sintani*, a term common between sisters-in-law, and now that she had a child Nasaba referred to her as Mother of Alberto.

There was something rather special about Morissa and I felt Lpiritian ought to be glad he had her for a wife, yet when I praised her qualities he merely said 'Thank you' and would never be drawn to comment further. She had a remarkable presence which, when she was not brimming with laughter, struck me as being at one and the same time both matronly and regal. She had a strong face, open and honest, twinkling eyes and slow, graceful movements which Alberto had obviously inherited from her. Although she was subservient to her husband's needs as the rules of the tribe required her to be, the knowledge that he could not manage without her endowed her with an air of independence. She was the mainstay for all Lpiritian's interests and indulgences, and I could see that as the family grew she would become the pivotal point and focus of the household. Morissa had not joined us for the circumcision ceremony. It was her place to remain in the village with those women who did not have sons of eligible age. When we had returned from the *lorora* I had wondered how she felt about losing the adorable Alberto to her mother-in-law. How much did she really miss him, and was her loss tempered by the fact that another child was on the way? It was one of those questions which was to remain unanswered.

Even though I could not converse with Morissa it was evident from her demeanour that she was genuinely pleased to welcome me as a guest. She seemed to find a white man a source of great curiosity, and I frequently caught her staring quizzically at me. I doubt whether she had ever seen a *mzungu* at close quarters before, still less entertained one in her *ngajii*. She was attentive to all my needs. I suppose to her I was seen in the light of a senior elder. Whenever we returned from an excursion the fire was immediately stirred into life and she quickly presented us with mugs of tea, beaming delightedly when I indicated I could drink a second one.

With no house cow of her own, Morissa had only the milk from her goats to rely upon. As milk was in such short supply she prepared either rice or *posho* for us to eat, bought from Lpiritian's earnings. Although I was glad to eat the food as a welcome change from the blood and milk of the *lorora* it augured ill for the tribe. Such food would have been unthinkable a few years ago, and its acceptance now was an indication of the damage done to the Samburu economy by the drought. Their culture, indeed their very existence, was dependent upon their cows. It was the love of their cattle which more than likely drove them south into Kenya, unable to withstand the desiccation of their former homelands. Always living on the edge of survival, they had been content with the marginally better grazing offered them by the land below Lake Turkana, the land they now occupied. But the drought had caught up with them and the rainfall was faltering, even in this area, creating the same arid desert land they had fled from. Left to their natural inclinations they would have followed the rainfall and pushed further south, but the constraints imposed by a nation of permanent dwellers who claimed ownership of the land on which they lived meant these nomads were trapped within the boundaries of what was now regarded as their territory.

To an outsider like myself, there appear to be three options open to them. To forsake their beloved cattle for camels like the Rendille who border them to the north-east, to forgo their nomadic lifestyle to join the growing number of Kenyans eking out a meagre living by cultivating the land, or improving the quality, not the quantity, of their herds and engage in water conservation projects with government support. For a short while some of the tribe chose a fourth and futile option; that of raiding cattle from neighbouring tribes with considerable loss of life.

Morissa invariably presented the food she prepared for us in a large metal washing-up bowl. It was handed to me first so that I could eat my fill before the remainder was consumed by Lpiritian. Morissa never ate with us.

One evening as we sat outside the *ngajii* in the gathering dusk, Lpiritian looked up from the bowl as he rounded off the last handfuls of food.

"It's a jolly good thing I have been through the *lminong* ceremony, otherwise we could not have eaten food prepared by *mparatut*. Nor could we have eaten in the *nkang*."

I was surprised by these comments, and Lpiritian began to

explain. "You see, I am still bound by the rules of warriorhood which prevent me from eating in front of a woman or consuming food prepared by one, until the *lminong* ceremony has been performed. It usually takes place after the first child is born rather than when a couple marry. Normally it marks the occasion when an elder, newly elevated from the warrior age-set loses his long braids. But for me that momentous event had already passed as my employers made me wear short hair when I started work at the Safari Lodge. Nevertheless my head was shaved and the elders arrived to take tea outside my wife's *ngajii*.

"The ceremony itself took place inside the hut. Two elders from my father-in-law's *lajii* sat round the fire while three of my closest friends, together with me and my wife, sat in the sleeping area. The elder sprinkled tobacco on the fire as a kind of incense, filling the hut with acrid fumes while they prayed to Nkai to bless the house and to bring us children, wealth and good health. My wife was then told to give me milk to drink which I did, spitting on my chest three times in blessing.

"It was a very simple ceremony but it filled me with emotion because that was the first time I had eaten anything in front of her. It also marked the end of all those years since I became a warrior and had to prepare food for myself. The elders then commanded her to look after me properly and to feed me with care for the rest of my life. You know, it really is a good thing to have a wife to do that for you, and I appreciate every meal she makes for me."

It seemed very strange that Lpiritian and Morissa had been married for more than a year before they had eaten in sight of each other, but marriage for the Samburu is a gradual process which gathers shape over a period of time. The presentation of cattle as bride wealth to the bride's family, circumcision of the bride and the slaughter of a sacrificial bull to signify the marriage contract all take place within a day. The circumcision of girls is watched only by other circumcised women in the village and is performed at the entrance of the mother's house. As in other Samburu ritual ceremonies, the doorway must face a holy mountain. There is no shame if the girl cries out or shows pain. After the ceremony she is laid to rest on a raised bed until she recovers from her ordeal.

The following day is also momentous in that the bride, now wearing her marriage necklace and ochre-covered goatskins leaves her family for the last time. As she departs from the *nkang* she walks between a guard of honour of elders standing with crossed staffs to form an archway. She sets off for the groom's village, accompanied by her husband and his best man.

It is a journey which has to be accomplished in a day no matter how far the destination, and on account of her circumcision she will need to rest a great deal on the way. On arrival at the groom's village she is promised her own livestock, and this will be presented to her on the following day. The wedding ceremony is then concluded. However the marriage itself is not consummated for a further three or four weeks during which time the couple will sleep in the groom's mother's house. Once the bride is healed, the couple will sleep alone and the mother will be told to move elsewhere. Thereafter it will be at least another four weeks before the bride builds a home of her own, helped on the first occasion by all the other women in the village.

On the day of the wedding both the bridegroom and his best man wear coiled brass earrings normally worn by married women. Once when Lturungen was staying with us in Nairobi, we drove past a group of Maasai driving a number of cattle ahead of them. Lturungen surprised me by announcing the party was on its way to a wedding. At the time I wondered how he had known that when we had no more than a fleeting glimpse of them. But he had caught sight of the earrings. Later I came to realise that beads and other ornaments, and even hairstyles, are not worn haphazardly but are part of a complex visual language which conveys not only the status of the individual within a tribe, but also indicates the fortunes of his or her family.

You can tell a Samburu boy who has not been circumcised by

the green necklace he wears and the 'pudding-basin' hairstyle. In the weeks before his circumcision, Karaito wore a *nchipi*, eight strings of blue beads hanging down the back of his neck and terminating in wing covers of a beetle. His hair was shaved off all except for a circular patch on top of his head. Later his mother adopted the green and blue beads to indicate she had a son who was recently made a warrior, and subsequently she would wear a double strand of dark blue and white beads for each of her warrior sons.

Strings of pale green and blue beads worn as a necklace indicates a woman has given birth. Two cowrie shells round the right arm signifies the wearer is a twin, and a string of black and white beads is worn by a warrior from the left shoulder and across his heart until such time as he has a sweetheart and presents them to her. Elders wear virtually no beads at all, but a shaven head indicates a turning-point in the fortunes of his family, and thongs of lion skin tied below the knees signify special occasions such as his *lminong* ceremony or a son elevated to the warrior age-set. Younger people often wear bracelets around their ankles. The little square of leather attached to a cord around Lturungen's right foot was a sign that his mother was living, and the absence of one on his left foot informed me his father was dead.

The most favoured ornament of all is the *njilii*, which adorns the forehead of so many Samburu warriors and women. Nowadays cut from sheet aluminium, it is in the form of a cross based on the four faces of a pyramid. No one seems to know its origin.

When he was in England our Pokot friend, Lokwang, had alerted me to the habit of the nomadic tribes of sharing their belongings. It had caught us off our guard at first. The boy was open and honest in all his dealings and I had no reason to doubt his integrity, yet he would help himself to any item of clothing he fancied. Our daughters were incredulous when he set off for school wearing one of their sweaters, or more frustratingly, some of their jewellery. There were several mornings when we felt we were about to have a riot on our hands and only narrowly persuaded them from lynching him, yet everything he borrowed was always returned exactly as he had found it, and nothing ever went missing. Later we realised he didn't appreciate he was doing anything out of the ordinary.

In the day or so Lturungen had spent in Nairobi with our friends prior to our arrival, the family went through the same anguish. He too helped himself to things belonging to others and more significantly, such personal items as toothbrushes and other toiletries. I was therefore well prepared for the experience of communal sharing when I went to live with the Samburu. One day my shoes would go wandering off to Archer's Post. On another day a shirt would be out in the plains adorning a warrior. By now Lturungen was well aware of these differences in outlook, and between us we took steps to safeguard two valuable items of equipment I had brought with me, he taking care of the tape recorder while I made sure that the camera stayed out of the reach of others, not through a lack of generosity but in the knowledge of the damage which could be caused unwittingly if they got into the wrong hands.

On one occasion when we were walking past a village I caught sight of some young boys throwing cow dung at the walls of a *ngajii*. I was taken aback by this unruly outburst; it seemed at odds with the orderly behaviour of the youngsters I had seen elsewhere. "What's going on?" I asked Lturungen.

He smiled. "It is terribly unlucky if a woman has no children," he said. "There will be nobody to look after her in old age. That house must be occupied by a woman who is childless. That is why they are throwing dung at it. Let's have a look."

The boys were surprised to see us and ceased their activities for a moment. One of them showed me a little mud and dung 'baby' he had made, presumably at the woman's behest, and which he was going to present to her. Apparently slinging dung at her house was the first part of the ceremony. The boy who had made the figure explained that he would return the following week and on that occasion the woman's husband would kill a bull. When it had been cooked and eaten the boy would rub a little of the fat on the woman's stomach saying "May Nkai give you a child".

I thought it curious that such young boys should be saddled with this kind of responsibility, and more so that a married woman was prepared to accept their participation in such a personal matter, but Lturungen was quick to remind me that in his tribe everybody had their duties and responsibilities. *Nkanyit* was the order of the day, and everybody including the youngest child was accorded respect.

"Does it really work?" I enquired.

Lturungen insisted that it often did, but I somehow felt he was less convinced than he had been when he had described to me the power of the curse.

Life in the *nkang* followed a gentle rhythm. Everyone went about their business at a leisurely pace. Time had little significance. A full moon marked the most auspicious occasions and governed the pattern and frequency of Samburu ceremonies. With no day of rest, the passing of weeks went unnoticed. Dawn and nightfall served to separate one day from the next, and the heat of the sun rather than the hour determined the course of the day. I found freedom from the tyranny of the clock remarkably refreshing. Motivation remained, but the tensions and anxieties associated with accomplishing tasks in a given period of time were entirely absent. It made me realise how these people had come to live in the state of 'now', cocooned in the present and unadulterated by the woes of yesterday and the worries of the morrow. Perhaps that explained in part why Morissa did not appear to grieve for Alberto during the weeks he lived with us at the *lorora*.

CHAPTER TEN

Circumcision — *Muratare*

brass earring

CIRCUMCISION FOR the young men of the Samburu is a test of bravery and resolve. It is their only means of admittance to adulthood. The *lakitoni* — as the circumcisers are called — are relatively few in number and travel long distances to perform the operation.

The operation itself usually takes between one and three minutes per initiate, depending upon the skill of the circumciser and the sharpness of his knife. It is performed without anaesthetic in full view of the warriors and elders of the tribe. The foreskin is retracted and the inner skin attached to the glans is severed. It is then pulled forward and a small slit is made in the top of the prepuce. The glans is pushed through the slit so that the prepuce hangs below the penis in the form of a tag.

As a test of bravery and self-control, each candidate is obliged to remain absolutely motionless while the operation is performed. Even an involuntary twitch or the blink of an eyelid would be a disaster. It would be interpreted as a sign of cowardice, bringing great shame not only to the candidate, but to his family, the other initiates and to his clan. He would be beaten hard in public. No other initiate would want to form a ceremonial friendship with him during his period of warriorhood, and the girls of the tribe would refuse to marry him. His parents would cover their hair with ashes and others would immediately drive his father's cattle straight through the thorn stockade surrounding the encampment, not only wounding them but scattering them on the plains. Thereafter all visitors to his mother's *ngajii* would enter backwards as a sign of contempt for the family. The shame heaped upon his relatives, and indeed the community as a whole in these circumstances, is unimaginable.

"You have to grow up as a Samburu from boyhood to understand what circumcision means to us," Lturungen once said to me. "No outsider could possibly understand how we feel about it."

His comments did not surprise me. I had noted how, on various parts of his body, his skin was defaced by round scars the size of inoculation marks. The Samburu often scarify their bodies as a means of decoration, but these marks formed no particular pattern. When I asked Lturungen how he had obtained them he explained it was common for young boys to put burning sticks or small wads of burning cloth on their arms and legs to see how well they could withstand the discomfort in preparation for the pain of circumcision which was to follow in later years.

It seemed to me the Samburu attitude to circumcision was something of a paradox. In the day to day organisation of their lives, the tribe paid heed to neither the past nor the future. They lived only for the day, thereby minimising their propensity for fear or worry. Therefore it seemed irrational that they should devote so much contemplation to this one event in their lives, years before it took place. There was no doubt in my mind that the fear of failing oneself, one's family and one's clan during the circumcision ceremony was an infinitely greater ordeal to the initiate than bearing the pain of the operation.

As the day appointed for the ceremony approached, tension mounted throughout the *lorora*. It appeared to affect everyone — parents, brothers, sisters, warriors and elders. Lpiritian in particular felt a great weight of responsibility upon his shoulders because, as head of his family, it was he who had decreed that by far the youngest initiates, Karaito and his half brother Lobuka, should be put forward for circumcision before the current age-set closed. Many believed the ordeal would be too great for them.

Lpiritian had to balance the psychological effect on the two youngsters of delaying circumcision until the next ceremonies were held in the year 2004 against the chances of them failing to meet the challenge of initiation now. Yet another consideration was whether they would be mature enough to survive on their own in the bush during the initial years of warriorhood at a time when they were still only boys, and lacked the determination and strength of young men. Lpiritian, always calm and calculating, had pondered on the matter for a long time before reaching the decision to offer them to the knife at such a tender age.

Preparations for the ceremony are put in hand a month or so before the event takes place. First of all the *lorora* is built. The elders choose a site on open level ground within easy reach of the surrounding woodland which is needed for firewood. More care is taken over the construction of each hut than is usual in a village encampment, and the rules relating to the construction of the *lorora* are carefully observed. The *ngajijik* are arranged in strict order of seniority, both within the clan and also within each family. Many husbands and older children remain at the *nkang* to look after livestock and the *lorora* is largely occupied by the mothers of the initiates and their youngest brothers and sisters, and a select band of elders.

Once the mothers have settled in they set to work to make cloaks for their sons to wear through the period leading up to circumcision and for the month afterwards before they are invested as warriors. Each cloak is made of three goatskins sewn together and then rubbed all over with a mixture of charcoal and animal fat to make them black. The boys wear them loosely knotted over one shoulder in the way that all skins were worn originally. Then their hair is shaved, leaving merely a circular tuft at the back of their heads, and they don the distinctive badge of initiates, the *nchipi* with its eight strings of blue, or blue and white, beads hanging down the back of their necks, and terminating in bronze-coloured beetle wing covers.

It is at about this time that the initiates begin to wander from *nkang* to *nkang* singing the *lebarta*. It is a soulful melody full of humility. The ditty is hauntingly beautiful, its dying cadences lingering in the ear. The words are simple, begging for meat to eat and imploring the elders to expedite circumcision, even though the boys know what an ordeal it will be.

Most Kenyan tribes practice circumcision. I recalled our Luyha friends and their custom of circumcision which takes place during the month of August every second year. One boy from their particular village was so terrified by the thought of initiation that he habitually vanished when the time for circumcision approached, hiding in the bush and sleeping in trees to appear only when August had passed. After each occasion the taunts from his friends grew more vociferous, until at last their ridicule became so unbearable that he felt it better to succumb to the knife than continue his subterfuge. Not so for the Samburu, with their discipline and strict adherence to tradition. Once a father has put his son forward for initiation there is no turning back and no means of escape. They know there is only one course open to them, the course which elevates them from being mere children with no standing in the tribe to the exalted position of a warrior. Little wonder they wanted initiation to come to them as quickly as possible.

The words of the *lebarta* were taken seriously. At a time when drought had decimated the livestock I was surprised to find how generous people were in offering up animals for these boys to consume. Since they had donned their black cloaks they had all gone from a diet consisting almost entirely of milk to one of meat. The elders slaughtered the animals for them, and the boys consumed huge quantities which they cooked in the bush out of the sight of women. I wondered how their bodies coped with such a sudden onslaught of solid food, and Lturungen confirmed they might well suffer from upset stomachs in the first few days of feasting. It was believed by the tribe that they needed this meat to build up both their nerve and their strength for the forthcoming ordeal, and also to counteract the loss of blood which it would entail.

"Nobody will ever dare to refuse these boys an animal if they ask for one," Lturungen said. "It is shameful to be mean. Besides, we believe that Nkai will be generous to those who give generously to others."

After some three weeks had gone by there came a morning when the boys were led out of the *lorora* by a group of firestick elders to collect sticks, staves and gum. These specially chosen men were in an age-set between junior elder and senior elder, and had been given the title of firestick elder at the beginning of the four-year period of circumcision when there would have been dozens of initiates instead of the mere five preparing for circumcision now. The act of kindling fire at the time the first initiates gathered gum brought the new age-set firmly under the firestick elders' control.

From that moment on they would be responsible for supervising the initiates of the age-set in their area during their passage through warriorhood, disciplining them and training them in the many skills and observances which had to be learnt during this period of their lives, and at the same time being responsible for their moral and physical welfare. As the four-year period of circumcision was now at a close, this was the last time they would supervise initiates but they still had many years ahead of them when they would train and discipline the warriors.

I watched the initiates set out on their journey at the first light of day. They were full of youthful energy and enthusiasm.

To an inexperienced observer it might have seemed as if these five boys were setting out on a casual jaunt. They revealed no hint of the strenuous journey ahead of them. The sticks and staves they had to collect were to be used to make bows and arrows and *rungus* for each of them. They were to gather the wood from the Kalama mountains which loomed large on the horizon in the early morning light. However, the gum with which they were to tip their arrows had to be collected from the Silalei trees of the *Commiphora* family growing in the mountains around Marsabit, some 200 miles away. Such a journey was to take them over a week to accomplish, walking fifteen hours a day in intense heat and sleeping rough in the bush at night.

It was a punishing regime for ones so young, and it was a foretaste of the training they would later undertake as warriors when they would learn to withstand the hardships of thirst, hunger and tiredness. Three of the boys had just reached puberty. Their limbs had started to strengthen and I felt they were fitted for the journey, but I was concerned for Karaito and Lobuka who were setting out on this venture in childish innocence. I hoped the firestick elders would be wise enough to treat them with sympathy if they got into difficulty.

There was a lull in the preparations for circumcision while they were away, and life in the *lorora* took on the more leisurely atmosphere associated with village life. Then late one evening when it was already dark and the cattle had gathered within the safety of the thorn hedge, the boys returned. They looked bedraggled and exhausted in their black cloaks, but they arrived singing the *lebarta* and carrying their gum and the sticks and staves over their shoulders. Despite their exhaustion, they were not allowed to disperse until they had been blessed. Karaito and Lobuka were almost too exhausted to speak. Each was given milk to drink, and then they slept soundly until late into the next day.

By this time it was approaching the middle of January and the moon was high and round in the sky. A *lakitoni* had been engaged and the day for the ceremony was set. Tension began to mount. The Kudu horn sounded frequently to summon the elders to meetings at which the details of the ceremony were discussed. The horns of the Greater Kudu, are held in high regard and are blown only on ceremonial occasions or in time of danger. Its booming note added to the sense of excitement and expectation, and the population of the *lorora* swelled visibly as elders foregathered from all the villages around. Warriors came in from the bush in great throngs, their hair carefully groomed, with many intricate orange-painted facial decorations, and the blades of their spears decorated with black pompoms fashioned from ostrich feathers.

The number of people converging on the *lorora* signified the importance of the event. It increased my concern for the boys. The ordeal would have been severe enough for them if they were to have shared it with the members of their immediate families, but now there would be dozens upon dozens of men of all ages watching for the slightest flicker of movement as they underwent the operation. Some spoke openly of their fears that Karaito and Lobuka would not withstand the test of circumcision and thus bring disgrace to the clan. Such doubts, voiced aloud, could have sapped the boys' morale. In fact it had the opposite effect. Both of them were so ashamed that others had such a low regard for them that it seemed to strengthen their resolve.

The day before the ceremony began by the firestick elders calling the five boys together and demanding that they confess to any occasion when they had slept with a circumcised woman, a circumstance strictly forbidden by the rules of the tribe. On this occasion it was no more than a formality which had to be gone through, for the boys were all so young no one seriously believed they would have transgressed. Had one of them been guilty, a fine of two calves would have been exacted from him and his father would have been shamed by not being blessed with the other elders at the time of circumcision.

Later in the day an area in the centre of the *lorora* called the *naapo* was cleared of dung, and ox hides were set out on the

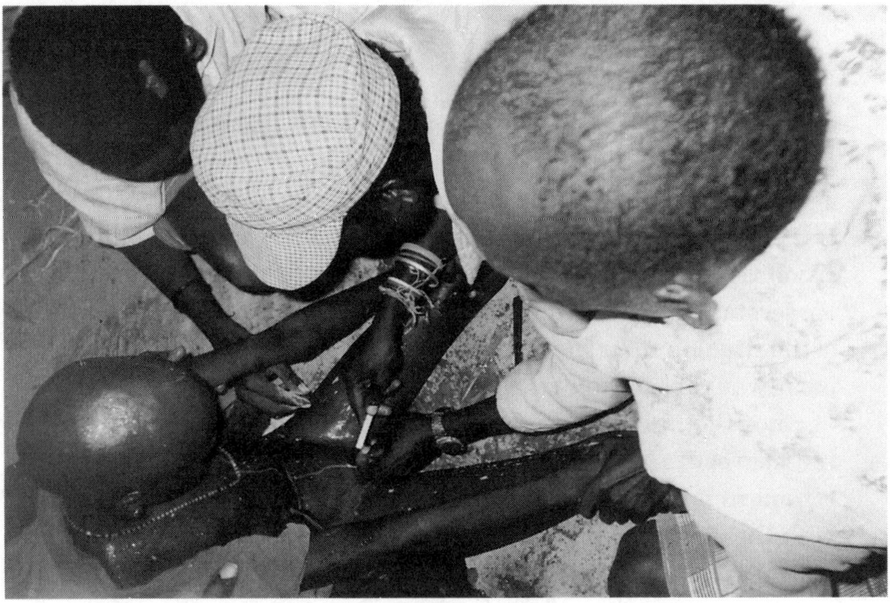

Karaito's circumcision

Lpiritian with Alberto

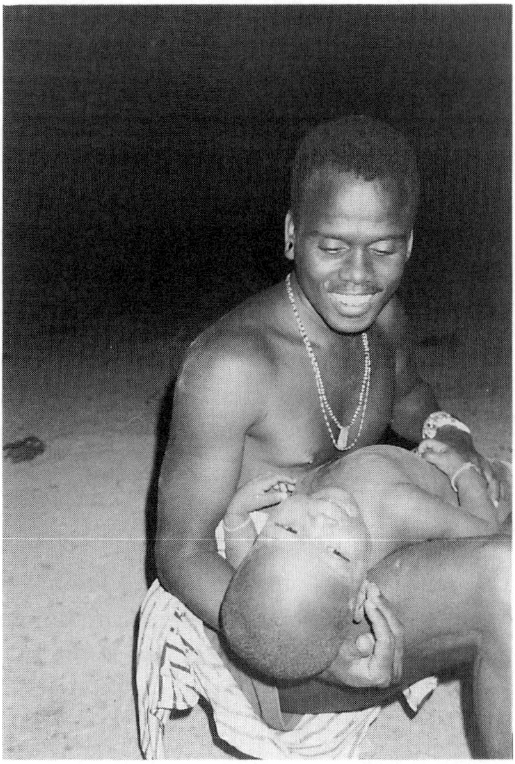

ground on which all the sharp tools of the households were placed and then blessed by elders by pouring milk over them. This blessing had a special significance for the initiates because it is believed it would help them withstand the pain of circumcision as well as ensuring their wounds did not turn septic. Understandably, Lpiritian could not vouch for the effectiveness of the ritual in reducing the pain of circumcision, but he assured me it was rare indeed for a wound to become septic.

Once the knives, *lalema* and axes had been blessed, it was the turn of the boys themselves to receive a blessing before they set out in a group to wash in running water and to bring back with them some of the water in small gourd-shaped containers which their mothers had recently hollowed out of lumps of wood. In some areas of the Samburu territory, running water can be many miles away with the result that the initiates are obliged to set out on another long trek. From our location, however, it was merely a matter of fetching water from the Wuaso Ngiro, a journey which could be accomplished in a few hours. As the boys returned to the *lorora* each entered separately through his family's stock gate, and as he did so his mother met him with a gourd of milk, and using a cow tail swab, flicked a little milk at his feet in blessing.

It was time for the boys to remove the *nchipi*, the blue beads they had worn for the past month, and hand them over to their mothers. It was a signal for their mothers to mix some of the water their sons had brought back from the river with a little milk to wet their heads before shaving them once more. Some of the boys ended up with mutilated scalps where an unsteady hand accidentally cut the skin during the process, but Karaito's mother, using merely a safety razor blade, never once drew blood.

By now the day was drawing to a close. When Karaito and Lobuka had both been shaved I followed them into the *lorora* again to watch their ceremonial sandals being made. They were cut from ox hides using a long knife in the shape of a spear blade. They were the ox hides on which the knives had been blessed earlier in the day, and the same ones on which the boys would sit when they were circumcised. In the lengthening shadows I watched the elders mark out the shape of their feet on the hide, and once the sole was cut out I observed the skill with which they trimmed off thin strips of leather, and then twisted and knotted them into the soles to strap the sandals to the feet.

There remained but once last ritual to be performed. A ram was slaughtered for each boy and a small flap of skin was removed and tied to the middle finger of his right hand. The rest of the skin was then carefully prepared for his use next day when it would be laid on top of the ox hide on which he would sit for his operation.

The warriors sang sporadically throughout the evening, but seemed unable to sustain their performance for long. The familiar resonance and vitality of their singing was strangely absent. As the evening wore on and tension mounted, several of them threw fits. It was an alarming sight at first; these strong and virile young men acted quite normally one moment, and the next charged out of control in a violent, hysterical outburst, oblivious of everything around them. On several occasions I saw them trip over bushes as they ran; their torsos and limbs became rigid and they had to be forcibly restrained by their comrades. Their breathing was disturbed, and they uttered a series of spluttering, bleating and groaning noises as if they had been possessed by a malevolent spirit. After some minutes the fits subsided. Those who had been attending them released their hold and helped them to stand again, although they remained dazed for several minutes more before they rather sheepishly rejoined their friends.

Although this phenomenon, called *ndokuna*, is very common amongst the warriors, some elders, and even occasionally women, I had assumed they would have been ashamed of it and was somewhat concerned when I caught Lturungen standing over a prostrate warrior with the microphone from my tape recorder pushed close to his face to capture the agonising sounds coming from his lips. I need not have worried; the tribe, it seems, regards these outbursts as a sign of manliness, and no one was the slightest bit perturbed by Lturungen's intervention.

That night no one slept very well. As I lay on my cow hide I became aware of a restlessness which filled the *lorora*. The cattle seemed constantly on the move. Warriors were wandering about in the dark. Every now and again I caught snatches of agitated conversation as they roamed to and fro among the *ngajijik*. Karaito stirred uneasily. The rhythmic breathing of sleeping people was strangely absent, and told me that the family was, like me, lying awake, their heads filled with the thoughts of the morrow. Little Alberto was the only one of us oblivious of the events to come.

At the outset I had distanced myself from family concerns about the forthcoming circumcisions. I was, after all, only a bystander with no ties of kinship. I had come merely to observe a ritual which had been carried out thousands of times over many generations on countless individuals, and which had no significance as far as my own life was concerned. When the events had run their course I would return home and resume my own style of living. Distance would both shield and separate me from the consequences of any shortcomings on the part of the candidates. Yet as the days rolled on and the time for circumcision approached, I found myself drawn irresistibly into the tensions building up all around.

So much kindness and consideration had been shown me by my hosts, and our daily lives were so intertwined that I could not avoid identifying with them and sharing their concerns. The two young initiates knew it was their forthcoming elevation to warriorhood which had led me to live amongst them. They came to regard the presence of a *mzungu* as a welcome adjunct to this momentous event in their lives, and empathy grew between us. I admired too what Lpiritian had put into the arrangements for an event which at this time of drought would cost him dear in terms of animals, hides, clothing, beads and even the quantity of red ochre which would be consumed. I desperately wanted the occasion to go well for his sake, more especially at a time when he was still establishing his credibility as head of the family. If Karaito and Lobuka failed him now, he would forever feel the guilt of having put them forward at such an early age.

I had greater confidence in Karaito than Lobuka. Karaito wore his sensibilities on his sleeve. He was brash and confident, almost over-confident, and was keenly aware of the impression he made on others. Although he lacked concentration I believed he could steel himself long enough to withhold all emotion until the operation had been performed, even though he might sob his heart out later on his newly constructed cot in the confines of the *ngajii* when it no longer mattered.

Lobuka I was not so sure about. I felt I knew him less well. He was shy and retiring and said little. He acted as Karaito's shadow, always in his presence but three paces behind; always at the scene of action but leaving Karaito to make the running. He had survived the gruelling trip to fetch gum remarkably well, but I wondered how effectively he would perform when he faced the knife alone outside his mother's doorway, the last of the boys to be circumcised and with a throng of people looking on.

The more I thought about the circumstances facing these boys and the retribution which would arise if their resolve failed them, the more anxious I became. It seemed as if sleep would never come, and yet I must have dozed for I remember being woken by the sound of rustling. Outside it was deathly still; no sound or movement from anywhere.

The first glimmer of dawn was visible through the window, and the sound I heard was Karaito getting up. Within minutes we had all left our beds. This was not a morning like other mornings; there was no tea to wake us and the cattle would remain in the *lorora* until all the circumcisions were completed. When I went outside into the still air, the cattle stood calmly — all of them — as if they too knew the significance of the day ahead. The sky itself reflected the mood, for a bank of cloud obscured the sunrise.

Each candidate stood patiently outside his mother's hut. The women and children retreated within, and the warriors and elders who were wrapped in their *nangas* against the coolness of the morning stood around in subdued conversation in the grey light. Already one or two of the *lmurran* had suffered fits, to be followed later by one of the fathers, their whooping and bleating sounding all the more frightening in the hushed atmosphere. Then the *lakitoni* appeared. He was a dapper fellow sporting a new pale cream cloth cap and a smart white shirt. Although elders wear almost no ornaments they have a liking for hats. I had seen everything put to use from a shabby bowler to the utilitarian beret. The *lakitoni* was much respected and well paid, and his new cap and shirt were a symbol of his prosperity.

We didn't go to see the other boys being circumcised but waited instead with Karaito and Lobuka, both of whom stood quietly showing no sign of emotion. The other circumcisions had gone well and barely ten minutes had passed before the *lakitoni* was striding towards us.

Karaito's two sponsors, who were junior elders and who would become as godparents to him, immediately laid the ox hide on the ground and placed the sheepskin pad on top of it. They removed Karaito's cloak and sandals, and he stood naked on the ox hide. The water he had collected from the Wuaso Ngiro the previous day was mixed with milk and poured over his head, whereupon he plummeted to the ground, sitting on the sheepskin pad with outstretched legs apart and his hands resting on his thighs.

Lerantilei and Lekalaile, his two sponsors, held his back and his right leg respectively but, instead of looking steadfastly forwards as most initiates do, Karaito sat with his head down. In consequence he could not avoid seeing the progress of the operation. The *lakitoni* picked up his knife and knelt down for action. My heart was in my mouth. This was no longer the flamboyant Karaito, but a child submitting meekly to an age-old custom —

a custom which could heap honour and glory on him or alternatively bring him disgrace and shame. Was it right that a mere child should have to undergo such an ordeal, I wondered? I would have done almost anything to help this boy through the next few minutes of his life, but it was an ordeal he had to undertake by himself. I remembered the camera in my hand. I hadn't the nerve to take a photograph, but instead pushed it into Lturungen's hands for him to operate.

I tried to imagine how Karaito's mother felt, hidden away inside her hut, while her son bared himself to the world outside and she unable to do anything to help him. I thought of her listening intently for the slightest murmur from the crowd which would indicate he might have disgraced himself, and the consequences it would have for her and her other sons.

As the *lakitoni* cut, so the blood welled up. I felt sick with worry. I tried to comfort myself in the knowledge that the operation was never as painful for a child as it was for an adult, and that as there were only five initiates to be circumcised the knife would remain razor-sharp throughout.

Within a couple of minutes it was all over, and the *lakitoni's* knife was being cleaned with milk and water. Karaito started to sing the *lebarta*, and with his body still wet from his dowsing Lerantilei and Lekalaile picked him up very gently and carried him, still singing, into his newly made cot.

I should have felt some relief, yet the tension persisted. The *lakitoni* moved swiftly on to his last candidate, Lobuka, and the onlookers moved with him and were joined by others involved in the earlier circumcisions. The throng was so large that they were obliged to stand in a huge arc before the *ngajii*. Lobuka sat staring unseeingly into the crowd. He seemed perfectly composed. Were my worst fears to be realised, or had he an inner reserve which had escaped my attention? He sat as still as a statue and could as well have been in a trance, his body absolutely frozen, until the operation was over. I sensed a communal sigh of relief. For a moment nobody moved. Then the crowd was ecstatic; the warriors let out whoops of joy and burst into song. The younger boys ran from their huts and prepared to take the cattle out to pasture, while the elders opened the gates of the stockade. There had been no need to drive the animals in fury through the thorn hedge, for the initiates had upheld the honour of their clan.

Suddenly all tension had dissipated and, as if in celebration, the sun climbed above the bank of cloud which lay in the east and bathed the plains in gold.

CHAPTER ELEVEN

Warrior-making: the Ceremony of Arrows — *Lmuget Loolbaa*

Lobuka shooting his arrows

LPIRITIAN HAD a smile on his face. Now that the initiations were over he had relaxed like the rest of us.

"You know how aggravating Karaito can be?"

"Yes."

"Well, he's not going to find the next month at all easy." He saw my look of surprise. "You see, we've absolutely forbidden him to upset anyone, and you know how difficult that will be. We Samburu believe that if a boy quarrels with someone between circumcision and warriorhood he will go on upsetting people for the rest of his life."

When he was at his worst, Karaito was like a bluebottle trying to find its way through a pane of glass. When something was not quite to his liking he buzzed around making a great commotion and upsetting everyone. Then he would speed off somewhere else and, just when you thought he had given up, he was back again as tenacious as ever. Keeping the peace with others was only one of many restrictions placed on the *laibartak* between circumcision and warriorhood. They were forbidden to use a knife, or pick up food with their fingers. Neither were they allowed to bathe, climb trees or wade rivers. They had to return home to sleep each evening and they were not allowed to drink water for the first two weeks. The reasons behind many of these restrictions were obvious. By returning home each night their parents could keep a check on the state of their health after their operation. Drinking blood and milk instead of water reduced the need to urinate, which meant they handled themselves less frequently, and the restriction on washing, wading and climbing reduced the risk of infection or of re-opening the wound.

Just now these constraints were not uppermost in Karaito's mind. He was lying in his cot with his legs splayed and wishing for the time to come when he had recovered enough to get up. During the morning a number of women paid their respects to his mother, and elders came to bless the household. Lpiritian, acting *in loco parentis*, celebrated the occasion by wearing a string of green beads round his head and a strip of lion skin tied below each knee like garters. Coiled copper earrings, which normally adorn married women, are worn by the head of the household on special occasions, and these now hung from his ears. In the meantime some of the women from the *lorora* had gone out to cut acacia branches, and returned to place a branch on either side of the doorway of the huts housing the newly circumcised boys.

By late afternoon Karaito felt well enough to get up, and walked around holding out his goatskin cape in front of him so that it didn't rub against his wound. Lobuka, too, left his cot for a while, and remembering his own circumcision at the even younger age of eight, Lturungen remarked upon the speed with which the younger ones overcame the operation.

Next morning, Karaito very gingerly washed away the dried blood from his wound, the only occasion on which he was allowed to use water, and then dried himself using some powdered chalk. Lerantilei and Lekalaile supervised him in this task, and then fashioned a bow and eight gum-tipped arrows from the materials he had collected from the mountains a week or so before. Finally they plaited his new headband from Doum palm fibres and decorated it with ostrich feathers. In the month to come, every bird that Karaito killed with his blunted arrows would be carefully skinned without the use of a knife, stuffed with grass, and then hung by its beak from his headband. No one, it seemed, could tell me the origin of this strange custom.

As the boys healed, so they again went about in a group singing the *lebarta* and requesting sheep to eat, which they roasted and then ate using sharp sticks in place of their fingers. On one occasion, when we feasted on *posho*, I showed Karaito how to use chopsticks. It wasn't difficult. *Posho* is thick and sticky when cooked and Karaito soon learned to eat as quickly with chopsticks as he could have done with his fingers. In fact he took a delight in racing us to the food and taking more than his rightful portion from our communal bowl.

As he began to heal Karaito's zest for life returned, yet he wasn't as bothersome as he had been before his circumcision. While he had obviously taken Lpiritian's admonition to heart, I believe he was also anxious to prove that even at his age he was capable of acting like a warrior.

January moved into February, and the moonless nights ended and the silver sickle of the new moon appeared in the sky. Karaito became impatient for the day when the ceremony of the arrows would be held, and the *laibartak* became elevated to warriorhood. His head was filled with thoughts of becoming a *lmurrani*, to discard his black cloak for a white *nanga* and adorn his head and shoulders with red ochre for the first time. He looked admiringly at the warriors as they sauntered through the *lorora*; their jaunty self-confident gait and their elegant coiffure intensified his desire to be one of them. These young men were his idols, and he longed for their life of liberty and adventure.

He and the other initiates were receiving regular instruction from the firestick elders. Karaito was determined to excel in the skills he was being taught. Now and again I would catch him off guard rehearsing dance steps, or practising the songs he would sing at his investiture. This boy's world was already mapped out for him. He had learned the songs and riddles of childhood; he knew the legends of the tribe, and was familiar with the tenets of Samburu life. He had passed through circumcision and had thereby elevated his status within the tribe. Warriorhood would take him a stage further. Then he would look forward to marriage, life as an elder, and hopefully become the owner of many head of cattle.

In common with Lmunyaki and Lobuka, Karaito had not been to school, could not read or write and had never even seen a building other than the little mud and dung huts his tribesmen lived in. Bricks and mortar, television, pens, pencils and paper were unknown to him. He had no need of formal education; he was already fully fitted for the world in which he lived. All the same it seemed strange to me, and yet in a curious way reassuring, that lively and intelligent youngsters like these living within reach of a school and not so very far away from a small trading post, should turn their backs on the very things most young people clamour for, and settle instead for a way of life so old that it stretched back to the roots of mankind.

"What can I bring Karaito as a present from England?" I had written to Lturungen.

"Nothing," he had replied. "There is nothing he will want", and I felt he had brushed aside my genuine desire to mark his brother's elevation with a gift, as if I were naïve to suppose there was anything in the wide world outside his tribe that a Samburu could possibly want. It brought home to me how complete in themselves these people were. Even the packets of sweets I had brought with me for the youngest children were rejected. Again, in my naïvety, I had not realised that as they had never come into contact with sugar these toddlers would find such delicacies unpalatably sweet.

As the moon waxed, so the warriors and the young unmarried girls began to descend on the *lorora*. They gathered like bees around the hive. Yet there was delay in settling the day of the ceremony, and when it seemed to have been fixed there was an inexplicable delay of a further day.

The night before the *lmuget loolbaa* the *lorora* was alive with dancing and singing. It began in the clearing in the centre of the *lorora* about an hour after dark. Spears twirled above the heads of the dancing warriors, and glinted in the light of an almost full moon. The throbbing virile columns of young men advanced and retreated to stamping feet, and a sonorous rasping sound which they expressed deep in their throats was interspersed with spasms of strident singing. From the other direction came columns of young girls in full voice, their harsh refrain repeated over and over again, their bead collars rising and falling as they jerked their necks forward in rhythm with the dancing, their heads raised and eyes closed as if in ecstasy. The columns gyrated, came together, moved apart and came together again. Each column sang separately, moving forwards and back so the sound of singing came in waves. The earth trembled with the movement of bodies; dust rose and the air quivered. All around bodies heaved and swayed, and perspiration glistened on the chests and arms of the men. Beyond, was the glow of hearths beside the perimeter huts, and the faint outline of the thorn hedge, and beyond again the silent brooding plains.

I must have stood and watched for an hour and more before I felt Lturungen tugging at my arm. Isaac was at his side.

"Quick," he said, "I want you to go back to the *ngajii* with Isaac. No one is there except for my mother and little mother (the name he used for his father's third wife). I want you to tell my mother exactly why it is I cannot live with the tribe. Tell her why I can't marry. Tell her how much my foot hurts. Tell her how much I miss my dad when I am left alone here. Make her understand!"

There was fervour in his voice. "Isaac will translate for you.

She will trust him. She will never believe me — she will say I am making it all up."

I was taken aback. He held my arm tight and started to walk me in the direction of the *ngajii*.

"Please, Roger, please do this for me. I have waited all this time for a chance for you to be alone with her. There won't be another opportunity before you leave us."

I was aware how little regard his mother had for him, but I had not realised it mattered so much to Lturungen. His desperation filled me with compassion. Here was one last opportunity to try to make amends with his mother, and I felt he had placed a great weight of responsibility on my shoulders. There was nothing I could do but to consent to his wishes.

The sounds of the celebration fell away in the distance as Isaac and I walked back to the *ngajii*. Lturungen's mother and little mother were sitting quietly beside the glowing embers. They must have wondered why we had come, but expressed no surprise — not even the mildest curiosity. I sat down at right-angles to them with my back supported by the wall of the hut, and Isaac sat opposite me. I had learned that when you have something important to impart you never face a Samburu directly, but speak looking past them or to one side. I gathered my thoughts.

I knew Isaac; he was trustworthy and discreet, and furthermore he had a good command of English. I could rely on him. Even so, I wondered what he would make of the revelations he was about to hear. I recalled the time Lturungen poured out his life story to me in the garden in Nairobi, and I drew on this pitiful tale for inspiration.

I began to speak, choosing the words carefully so that I should not offend. I explained why Isaac and I had come and my wish to talk to her about her son out of his hearing. I spoke about the pain he endured with his foot, the grief he still felt for the death of his father, his dislike of being touched by people, and the reasons why he preferred to be treated as an outcast rather than marrying. Remembering his mother's opposition to him going to school, I talked of the advantages of education for one who was crippled, and the opportunities it could offer him in earning a living away from the tribe.

However much Lturungen's story may have surprised — even shocked him — Isaac showed no sign of it, but instead struggled manfully to translate the complex concepts I had to put across to this ageing woman. On several occasions Lturungen's mother wagged her head to express surprise, and when I talked about Lturungen's foot she complained he walked about too much, saying his problem was his restlessness and not his foot. When I explained the reason I believed Lturungen disliked being touched by people and the consequences it had for his marriage she muttered 'Eh-eh' in understanding. Throughout I tried to convey the severity of Lturungen's plight, and his need of forbearance from his one remaining parent. Little mother sat listening, but said nothing.

After I had finished Lturungen's mother sat for a while with her arms clasped round her knees and rocked to and fro. We sat in silence — all four of us. Then at last she spoke.

"He's no help to us," she said, "we can't use him here. He has nothing to offer the *Loikop*. Take him away with you when you go. Take him back to where you come from and keep him."

I realised that I had failed Lturungen miserably.

Next morning we drank our tea as usual, opened the stock gates in readiness for the animals being taken to pasture, and waited for the events of the day. Five goats were kept back from the herd. They were to be slaughtered in place of cattle which were normally used on this occasion, since so many had died in the drought. Indeed it was Karaito's mother who had given him the traditional gift of a cow at his circumcision ceremony because Lpiritian, as the rightful donor, had no cattle to spare.

Presently the five *laibartak* appeared. They each had with them their two guardians who would care for them during the initial years of warriorhood — warriors who had been initiated at the outset of the new *Lmooli lajii* in 1990. They had experienced four years of life in the bush. The goats were separated and led individually through the stock gate of each initiate and out into a cleared area beyond. I had come to know Karaito's two guardians, Jonathan and Longoloto, from their frequent visits to the *lorora* and I felt they were well suited to look after their new charge. Each goat was thrown to the ground, and while one warrior held the feet, the other cupped his hands over its mouth and nostrils. Suffocation is a favoured means of slaughtering small animals. No violence is involved, and furthermore the skin remains undamaged. However murderous the Samburu may have been in days gone by when they plundered cattle, I had yet to see one mistreat an animal.

It seemed as if these little animals knew it was their duty to be sacrificed. They struggled half-heartedly and made no real attempt to escape. Gradually their movements grew weaker and their panting subsided. Within three minutes it was all over, and each goat lay prostrate on the ground.

Longoloto went to pluck some dried bushes, and together he and Jonathan laid the carcase on them. Jonathan took on the task of cutting up the animal. He could not have been more than seventeen or eighteen years old. His skin was very dark; he wore his hair in several pigtails bound round with fibre which hung down the centre of his back. Always quiet and composed he said little and thought much, and although he was gentle in speech and movement, with large fathomless eyes, I formed the impression that he could be a force to be reckoned with when his anger was raised.

I watched him take up his *lalem*. Using the tip of the blade he slit the goat carefully along the chest and belly. Despite the size of his sword he wielded it with precision, cutting the difficult bit round the tail with the neatness of a tailor. Then he peeled back the skin, separating it from the flesh, and the two warriors knelt and drank the warm dark blood which gathered in the fold. Although I did not mind blood with the coagulant removed, drinking fresh blood from a dead animal was something I could never have done. Lturungen knelt beside me, and when the animal was opened up he slipped his hand inside and pulled out a still-warm kidney. Using his knife he gave half to Jonathan and ate the rest himself with relish. It was an inexcusable thing to have done. Custom decrees that children, girls, married women, warriors and elders all have their allotted parts of an animal, and the kidneys were the delicacies which should have been reserved for the youngest children.

I admired Jonathan for the way he butchered the carcase. He had a thorough knowledge of the animal's anatomy and carried out his task with virtually no mess. Each part of the body was separated and carefully set aside to await its allotted owners. Some cuts of meat went to the sponsors who had held Karaito's back and leg during circumcision, and some to the elders. The chest, front right leg and shoulder went to Karaito and his guardians, and much of the leftovers including the head, neck and stomach were claimed by the women and children. The guardians of one of the other initiates who had spent some time at school were not so experienced in the art of butchery. They made slow progress with their animal, and were roundly denounced by the 'true' warriors and junior elders. From the invective I realised these two were regarded very much as second-rate *lmurran*.

Meanwhile Karaito created a fire, first bringing a burning stick from the embers outside his mother's hut which he placed on the ground near the remains of the goat. Then he piled kindling and larger sticks upon it. Each initiate had to dig a large fireplace some way off in the bush. The position and size of each trench had been marked out for them on the ground, and they then had to excavate the earth with their swords. Karaito was suffering from his usual lack of concentration; his progress was slow, and in the end he welcomed a hand from me. The small fire was then used to light a larger one in the trench. When there were only embers left, green sticks were placed across the trench and the meat laid across them and roasted. While all this was going on the mothers of the initiates collected their piles of meat in leather bags, and I saw they each wore around their necks the headdresses and birds which their sons had newly discarded.

The warriors made their own lair which was centred on a large tree some little way from the *lorora*. Once all the meat had been cooked there was frenzied dancing and singing, and the Kudu horn blew incessantly. Only the warriors, initiates and junior elders were present at this part of the ceremony. The senior elders were encamped some distance away in the centre of the *lorora*, and although I had been invited to join them, Lturungen, being conscious of his shortcomings as a tribesman, was too much in awe of them to take me there so instead I slipped into the guise of a junior elder and was made very welcome by the warriors.

Once the dancing had died down, each circumcised boy sat on the ground with his arms clasped round his legs, and was handed a piece of roasted fat. This he touched with his lips and then spat four times on his stomach in blessing. The warriors then took up the fat and smeared their charges down the righthand side of their bodies from head to foot. They changed positions, and the boys did the same to their guardians. The fat is called *nkiyeu*, and from that time on both initiate and guardian would refer to one another by the name of *nkiyeu*, signifying a special relationship which would last not only through warriorhood, but for the rest of their lives.

There then followed a test of strength, namely breaking a hip bone with a sword. Every initiate succeeded in doing this and it was not surprising since it is far easier to break the bones of a goat than those of an ox. Nowadays this ritual is regarded as a bit of fun. But a generation ago there would have been serious consequences if an initiate failed to break the bone at the first attempt.

The climax of the day was still to come. Karaito had to sever irrevocably his ties with his mother. Never again would he take food from her; from then on he had to feed himself in the bush. It would be some time after he was wedded before he was allowed to be seen eating by married women, or partake of food they had prepared. The only concession allowed him was to drink milk or tea in his mother's *ngajii*, but even that was permitted only so long as it was in the company of another warrior.

It was a simple but touching ceremony. Taking the top part of the broken hip bone, he presented it to his mother.

"Mother," he said in his clear boyish voice, "I am returning this food to you as a token of all that I ate with you when I was young." Handing it over to her, he ended. "You must never give me food again."

In a society plagued by drought and which lives on the edge of starvation this assertion of self-reliance, especially from one so young, was particularly poignant. His mother indicated her consent, and after Karaito had spoken I and his two elder brothers stood in silence at the doorway of the hut, and in our hearts we each hoped he would pull through when left to his own resources in the bush.

In the late afternoon when the day began to cool, we once again watched Karaito having his head shaved by his mother. He bent down on his knees in the doorway of her hut while she squatted beside him. The shallow seat of a four-legged stool was filled with milk and water. She wiped the mixture over his head with her hand, took off his beads and placed them in what remained of the mixture, and then set to work with her razor blade. Lpiritian's head was also shaved again, and once more he took up the green beads, copper earrings and the lion skin garters. When Karaito had been shaved, Jonathan and Longoloto covered his head with red ochre and daubed red on his arms and chest as well. He donned a new white *nanga* which is worn only for this occasion. Proudly he fetched Lobuka. The two of them went outside between the huts, and kneeling on the ground shot away their arrows at the little children who eagerly collected them as souvenirs. With this simple act they became warriors. Although they had no further use for the arrows, both boys kept their bows as they would need them in the months to come when they bled cattle.

More festivities followed. This time warriors advanced in

pairs ahead of the dancing column to see who could leap the highest into the air from a standing position, achieved by flexing the ankles rather than bending the knees. For the first time the five new warriors were allowed to join the others. They hung back at the rear of the column imitating the steps of their peers and looked extremely self-conscious.

A row of stools was set out for the senior elders who assembled and watched the proceedings from the sidelines. Lpiritian and I were invited to sit with them. These old men were there to make sure the ritual was carried out correctly. Muttering among themselves they used their *rungus* to point out good performers, and criticised the less able ones. The column danced into wind, and swirls of dust flew up behind. It was a fine sight to see, with each warrior carrying his spear in an upright position. Then it was the turn of the girls who advanced on the column from the other side of the *lorora* with their peculiar jerky movement which made the piles of bead necklaces round their necks leap backwards and forwards. After a while the warriors rested and the girls continued with singing, one soloist following after another in strident voices while the rest took up the chorus line.

I could see that Lturungen was ill-at-ease. Mindful of his dubious status within the tribe, he would not sit with the senior elders. Later on, when some junior elders began to dance I could see he longed to join them but was prevented from doing so by the condition of his foot. It was sad that one who had such a wide knowledge of his tribe's customs and practices and who had spoken so eloquently about them when he was in England, could not take part in the activities. He needed to feel there was a purpose behind his presence there, and when I handed over the camera and tape recorder and asked him to capture the atmosphere he accepted his commission gratefully.

Dancing resumed and the pattern changed, the warriors and girls performing in two long lines facing each other. Lturungen handed back my equipment and sought a partner, as did Isaac. They hunted far and wide amongst the girls who were without partners, but no one would dance with them, such was their disdain for these two who had been educated at school. So putting on a brave face they partnered each other. There was no holding of hands or touching between partners, but as the warriors danced so they flicked their long hair in a provocative manner in the faces of the girls they fancied.

Later that evening Lturungen and I stood impatiently in the moonlight by the family stock gate which had been left open on this auspicious occasion. We were waiting for the final celebrations to begin. In the distance we could see the fires the warriors maintained in their lair by the tree, and the night was punctuated by bursts of song and the sound of the Kudu horn. One of the songs, used only on this occasion, was extremely lewd. Lturungen refused to translate it, partly because he was embarrassed but more particularly because some of it was sung in code.

All over Kenya, and doubtless all over Africa, young people are attracted to the idea of a private language made up of words they have invented. Maybe it is the need to distance themselves from an adult society which exercises such a strict discipline over them that stimulates the younger ones to contrive a language of their own. I had noted how the children of our Luyha friends had invented a vocabulary to which only they were privy, and at one boy's boarding school in Nairobi the pupils have, over the years, built up a vocabulary and phrases which now amount to virtually a new language. Each Samburu age-set develops its own private language, and the current *Lmooli* age-set was no exception.

Much later than expected we heard the girls begin singing, proceeding from a gate on the far side of the *lorora*. Slowly they made their way round the outside of the thorn enclosure, and as they came towards the warriors' lair so the warriors advanced in a column to meet them, their voices faint at first and then growing stronger as they approached the open ground between their lair and the *lorora*. As they drew close the deep voices and the measured strain of the warriors provided a ground for the faster-flowing repetitive melody sung by the girls. The two groups of voices mingled and intertwined, and wafted out across the plains to the silent attentive Sabachi. Neither the majesty of the lion, noble though he is, nor the grandeur and might of the elephant, had anything to compare with the elegance and demeanour of these young mortals in their impassioned pursuit of their timeless ritual of courtship.

It was the early hours before Lturungen and I slipped into the *ngajii* to sleep, and still the sound of singing pierced the darkness. Next morning, Karaito and Lobuka returned to the *lorora* to be blessed at the stock gate by their mothers, and were accompanied by Jonathan and Longoloto. Then, picking up my rucksack, Lpiritian, Lturungen and I joined the four warriors and set off on safari, first to spend some time in their company and then to wend our way back to Lpiritian's *nkang*. As I left the *lorora* for the last time, Karaito's mother and her elderly companion were dissecting the stomach and head of the goat. One was engaged in the messy task of cleaning the entrails on a sheet of metal while, as I watched, the other took up her *lalem* and split the head down the middle between the eyes and ears, and flicked the brain out of the two halves.

Lpiritian carried the remains of a roasted leg of goat in his hand, and he ate the meat off it as we went along. After a while we stopped by a *lbaan* to wash and rest among large-leaved fleshy plants growing along its banks. A huge block of rock with a flat surface stood to one side of the *lbaan*, and Lobuka indicated that the four of them had spent the night there. Exhausted from the revelry they had stretched out and slept on that unyielding stone without even attempting to light a fire to fend off animals.

Somewhat shocked by this admission, I accused the two older warriors of being foolhardy. Longoloto hung his head and said nothing. Jonathan, who knew I admired him for his skills, was mortified. He maintained there were few dangerous animals in the area because the Shifta had killed so much of the wildlife.

"Besides," he assured me, "if a lion had attacked he would not have killed more than one of us because the rest would have woken with the noise, and we would have got away safely!"

CHAPTER TWELVE

Archer's Post

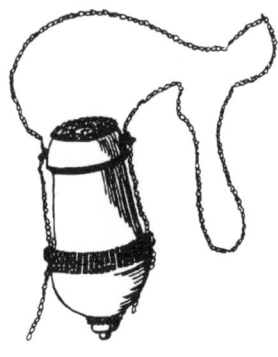

snuff container

MY LAST DAY with the Samburu dawned grey and sultry. The weather was changing. Lpiritian and Lturungen had insisted that I spend a couple of days with them in Archer's Post before I returned to Nairobi.

My few belongings were once more packed in the rucksack together with some items of clothing the boys wanted to take with them. A rucksack was of course a familiar object to Lturungen, but to the others it was an item of curiosity and the men, especially, were amazed I deigned to carry such a weight on my back. Although the womenfolk are obliged to collect and hump enormous loads of firewood, generally speaking it is unusual for the warriors and elders to carry anything more than a couple of spears, a *lalem* and a *rungu*, with perhaps a toothbrush stick tucked behind their ears. When we returned to the *nkang* from the *lorora* the men expressed concern at the weight carried by an ageing man over such long distances.

Filled with curiosity, Karaito attempted to lift the rucksack when it was leaning beside the *ngajii*, and gave up in disbelief. Lobuka just managed to raise it off the ground. In fact my belongings were so meagre, the rucksack was less than half full and light by normal standards. I soon discovered, however, it was impossible to wear a *nanga* and a rucksack at the same time. The *nanga* invariably worked loose through the action of the shoulder straps and ended up in a heap at my feet so that I was obliged to wear it only to waist height with a shirt on top.

Morissa, Ngalina and Nasaba and a variety of children gathered around us as we prepared to leave. My last memory of them is standing outside the *nkang* in a fit of giggles, with the rucksack on my back as I pretended to buck and bray like an irritable donkey under too large a load. We trekked westwards across land as level as a playing field, covered with a sprinkling of flat-topped acacias and low grey shrubs. There had been a very slight, almost imperceptible shower of rain in the early morning and now, as the sky cleared and the sun shone, I was aware of the aromatic smell reminiscent of crushed rosemary, given off by the bushes around, and which is so characteristic of the Samburu area when the land is not held in the grip of a drought.

We walked slowly. Lturungen's foot was raw and painful. The pain made him absent-minded, and his predicament was made all the worse because he had forgotten to bring his most comfortable pair of shoes with him. Indeed he seemed altogether unsettled, and I suspected he was becoming evermore conscious of the fact that our ways were soon to part.

After about an hour and a half we reached the main road north from Archer's Post as it struck out across the desert. Fearfully rutted between Isiolo and Archer's Post, it was in better condition here — a red trackway of crushed stone and grit standing proud of the surrounding plain by a couple of feet or more. Both the British and the Kenyan armies train in the area, robbing the Samburu of some of their best grazing lands. On the several occasions during my stay when we had come across a truckload of soldiers they had invariably been well-disposed towards the tribesmen, but I was told it was not unusual for people to be injured or maimed by live munitions left on the ground. There were the remains of a British encampment close to the road, and I was unimpressed by the bits of cardboard boxes, strips of metal and other debris strewn over the ground.

The road to Ethiopia, with a branch to Wamba and Maralal a little way north of where we stood, is like no other I know. We waited in the shade of trees for nearly three quarters of an hour before the first vehicle came into view. It announced itself as a cloud of dust on the distant horizon where Sabachi and Warges mountain appeared to march across the road. After a while we could see beneath the cloud some kind of object shining in the sun. Lpiritian reckoned it had raised too much dust to be a car. Eventually a snorting, throbbing, high-sided lorry of substantial proportions emerged out of its cocoon of dust. Lpiritian stepped calmly out into the road and signalled the driver to stop. The cab was already full of passengers. Lpiritian struck a deal with the driver, and for fifty Kenyan shillings we were permitted to hitch a lift on top of the load. Lturungen climbed up the ladder to find the lorry piled high with sawn logs. We passed up the rucksack and ascended ourselves. It was a rough ride, to say the least, and I soon realised my thin clothes were no protection against the rough-hewn wood. Every minute of that twenty-five minute ride was spent in anticipation of being pierced by a sliver in the backside.

Obligingly the vehicle pulled up at Archer's Post to let us off, shrouded in our own micro-climate of dust particles which followed at a respectable distance while we were on the move, but then engulfed us once we had stopped.

Founded as a forward post for the British administration by Geoffrey, later Sir Geoffrey Archer, this little trading community is an important crossing point on the Wuaso Ngiro. It is always given particular prominence on maps of Kenya, and because of that I imagined it to be a thriving, bustling frontier town. In fact the first time I arrived in the area, I had driven through it before I knew where I was. Fewer than twenty corrugated iron and wood shops and "hotels" face each other across the broad expanse of highway, and tucked behind are, at most, eighty tin and cement shacks, a small mosque, two diminutive churches and a rather larger Roman Catholic complex with church, school and clinic. There was a bar, a police station, army barracks and a water tower.

Life here runs at such a slow pace that it virtually stagnates. With so little traffic on the road, the area between the two lines of shops acts as a meeting place, especially at either end of the day when people stand around in conversation or indulge in some bartering in the cooler air. It is a cultural no man's land where no tribe dominates, and where tribal culture is suppressed by a quasi-Western veneer.

None of the tribes are at home here. Nomads like the Samburu and Turkana rub shoulders uneasily with those from the more settled Meru and Kikuyu tribes. Worldly-wise dealers in merchandise strike hard bargains with those whose wealth is counted in cattle and goats, and the conventions of nomadic life clash head-on with the principles of commerce. Yet Lturungen, notwithstanding his pastoralist background, possessed sufficient education, worldly knowledge and poise to move with ease between the traders, hotel owners, the church elders and the few settled pastoralists so as to be accepted by them all, whereas Lpiritian was very much the outsider. Only when it came to striking a bargain was Lturungen, with his inability to handle figures and relate monetary values to goods, hopelessly out of his depth, and it was then that Lpiritian, with cool deliberation, stepped in and clinched the deal.

The boys started off full of enterprise. The stay at Archer's Post was to be at their expense and I was to be their guest. As soon as we got off the lorry Lturungen dived into his friend's mother's lodging house to book us some rooms. Lpiritian and I followed him into a long, low store which was part of the establishment and which sold a miscellaneous range of goods and hardware. In one corner there was a treadle sewing machine on which the proprietress carried out rudimentary repairs to customers' garments. Behind the store and at right-angles to it lay a long courtyard lined on either side with breeze block rooms opening out onto a verandah. The rooms were no more than cubicles with a door and window and basic furnishings — a narrow bed, chair, table and hurricane lamp.

At this early stage in our stay the boys' plans began to go adrift. Inflation had taken its toll, and the price of a room was now 300 shillings a night. Even Lturungen was quick to realise that three rooms for two nights was more than twice the cash they had available to them. I attempted to intervene by giving them the money they needed, but they remained adamant that our stay should be their gift to me. Realising their predicament, the proprietress offered Lturungen the use of her son's room since he was away at the time, and Lpiritian resolved that he and I should share a bed between us.

It was some days since we had washed any clothes, and Lturungen was insistent that our laundry should be done without delay. He borrowed two plastic bowls into which we piled our washing, and after changing into civvies we left the rucksack in our room, padlocked the door and made for the river, crossing the mud flats below the shops. The wide expanse of dried mud and the profusion of rushes which grew up between the cracks was in stark contrast to the unremitting sand and rock I had grown accustomed to. When we reached the water it was running low and very muddy. By now Lturungen's foot was giving him real pain and he was reluctant to walk the 200 yards to the road bridge and the waterworks beyond. We suggested he abandoned the idea of washing clothes, but he pressed on with characteristic doggedness.

We crossed the bridge and found a hole through the perimeter fence of the waterworks. The grass compound inside had originally been a secure area for the employees, but, in characteristic African fashion, countless individuals bent on a supply of clean water for their washing had, over a period of time, worked away at the wire mesh enclosure until it was weakened and then finally broke. Now the locals behaved as if they had established a right to do their laundry there and with no funds available to repair the fencing, the officials could do no more than accept the situation.

Inside, water spilled from a large hosepipe and the grass was an oasis of green. Whole families were engaged in washing clothes. Lturungen produced a small packet of soap power from his trouser pocket. We filled the bowls with water and set to work. I had noticed in England that he had an aptitude for hand-washing garments, and he set to work with gusto on the contents of one bowl while Lpiritian and I shared the other. Our efforts did not accord with Lturungen's high standards. He was dismissive of our workmanship and we were soon relieved of our task and relegated to the menial duty of hanging the freshly washed laundry on the perimeter fence to dry. When all was done the boys filled the bowls with fresh water and made for the scanty cover of a clump of bushes just outside the compound where we stripped and washed and stood to dry within yards of the throng of people. By the time we had put our clothes on again the laundry too was dry, and we accompanied Lturungen on the slow and painful journey back to our lodgings.

By now Lpiritian was desperate for a drink, and insisted we paid a visit to the bar. It was a narrow enclosure which stretched towards the river, squeezed between two stores. It had a central walkway between trees and groups of tables and chairs partitioned off into alcoves with a rush roof above to offer respite from an unrelenting sun. Lturungen flitted from table to table greeting acquaintances while Lpiritian and I settled down to a bottle of beer each. Later Lturungen rejoined us, directing friendly banter at the other tables.

It could have been an orchestra with Lturungen as the conductor. Each group of tables was like a group of instruments, and Lturungen brought each of them into the conversation in turn. When the conversation become controversial they all participated, just as if the orchestra was playing fortissimo. Lturungen was not on good terms with everybody, however, and when one individual came and joined us at our table he froze, and I was once again subjected to the uncomfortable prickling sensation I experience when Lturungen is aware someone despises him.

We hadn't been at the bar long before someone swung his legs over the bench and gave me a friendly dig in the ribs as he sat down next to me. It was Buni. I expressed surprise. He guessed he would find us here and had driven his goats into town to join us, explaining he had parked them with a small child just down the river who was keeping a watchful eye on them while he joined us for a drink and wished me a safe journey home. It was a generous gesture. He must have walked with the animals for a good two hours, and I reckoned they deserved the rest as much as he did.

Lunch was taken in the largest and perhaps the oldest of the corrugated iron buildings. It was lofty and bare with a counter and a glass case at one end, and a sprinkling of wooden chairs and tables around the walls. The light flooded into the otherwise gloomy interior from two large doors, one of which opened off onto a yard at the rear and the other opening off the road. Lpiritian ordered lunch and insisted we washed our hands at the copper urn standing on a table in the yard. The food was plonked unceremoniously in front of us — a bowl each of an odd assortment of stewed bones, meat and gristle which we ate with our fingers — a hunk of bread, and water in none-too-clean glasses. It was hard work extracting the meat from the bone. The boys finished long before I did, and sat eyeing me critically. When at last I finished and felt pleased with what seemed to be a cleanly picked pile of debris, Lpiritian put me to shame by demanding my bowl and then proceeding to make another meal out of the left-overs.

Lturungen was exhausted by the pain from his foot, and not a little irritable that we could not undertake the programme he had planned for us. We left him to rest and made our way along a track which ran parallel to the river in the direction of the Samburu National Reserve. Some way out of the settlement we reached a *nkang* standing just back from the road with a view over scrubland to the river beyond. From its size it must have been the home of some seven or eight families. Erected on a wooden framework just inside the thorn hedge was a selection of Samburu artifacts displayed to catch the attention of tourists entering the reserve. Lpiritian longed to have a souvenir shop of his own as a means of providing for his family, and I realised it was his reason for bringing me in this direction. This was the first time I had seen Samburu work for sale, and Lpiritian was anxious to acquaint me with the sort of products he had in mind for his shop.

It was evident that these Samburu families had settled almost permanently and lived off their takings from tourists rather than from livestock. The women still dressed traditionally. Nevertheless they had lost much of their coyness and the children, too, exhibited little of their traditional respect for elders. A group of them swarmed around, surprised to see me in the company of one of their tribe rather than in a party of *wazungu*. I greeted them in their own language. They burst into surprised laughter, but rather than keeping a respectful distance they crowded around trying to persuade me to buy the objects on display. How long, I wondered, before they succumbed completely to a Western style of living and Western attitudes.

Lpiritian cast his eye over the racks. "What do you like here?" he asked.

Two items in particular had caught my eye. One was a necklace in the old style made from seed pods, simply decorated with small white circles. The other was a beautifully made snuff container designed to hang from one's neck, fashioned from a gourd barely four inches long, exquisitely engraved on the outside and with a close-fitting leather lid decorated with beads and a mother-of-pearl button. Fearing his generosity would outstrip his means I evaded Lpiritian's question. My subterfuge failed to work.

"You are a good friend. You are leaving us soon and I would

like to buy you a gift. And since you will not say what you like, I will choose something for you."

Without a moment's hesitation he picked the snuff container off the rack, but rather than handing it to me went off in search of the woman who had made it, and returned triumphantly a few minutes later to announce that he had negotiated a discount of thirty per cent.

Lpiritian was well known here. News of his arrival spread around the *nkang* and a tall, well-built and refined-looking individual appeared and greeted us in English. This was Lpiritian's friend and age-mate, Amos. He insisted we joined him for a beer in his *ngajii*.

It was larger than any I had been in before, with a separate compartment at the rear. We settled down on a cow hide. Beside us was a rusty metal chest which Amos opened, revealing it full of bottles of beer. Several others from the village joined us and the beer was handed round. I noticed, however, that traditional Samburu generosity and etiquette were breached, and Lpiritian was obliged to pay for the beer he and I consumed. Had we asked for milk instead, would that have come as a gift, I wondered?

Amos explained that trade from tourists was good and that the *nkang* was permanent even though they kept animals. He had sufficient income to use all the facilities offered by the trading post and he also sent his children to school. He liked the halfway house he maintained, living in the traditional style yet taking advantage of modern conveniences.

He and the villagers were still Samburu at heart, retaining an air of self-confidence and elegance which marked them off from the other traders, yet I could not help wondering what would happen to the children. Such regular contact with a settled population was wresting them away from their traditional lifestyle — a lifestyle they had barely known. School and education were prized by their parents, but where would it leave these youngsters who, because of their background, would still be saddled with the stigma of being Samburu by the rest of

Kenya? In a country with a booming population where too many were already searching for non-existent jobs they, like Lturungen, would suffer the trauma of having their expectations raised by an education which led them up a blind alley. Bereft of their traditional values and discipline and unable to advance in a world whose values were being imposed on them, another generation could see this village degenerating to an urban slum and the people no better than those poor souls who tried to eke out a living near the Catholic church by selling miscellaneous goods from little timber-framed booths with walls made from flattened tin cans, no more than six-foot square. Some served as homes as well. Amos was an honest and genuine person, and I had no doubt he believed he was doing the right thing for his family, yet like all Samburu he could not perceive what the future might hold.

Before we left, Amos asked me to take a gift from him to my wife. To my surprise he handed me the necklace which had caught my attention earlier. It seemed a remarkable coincidence to be given the very items which had impressed me most. If Samburu traders were able to match souvenirs to prospective purchasers as effectively as Lpiritian and Amos had done on this occasion, business should be very good indeed!

As we trudged home, the setting sun threw exaggerated shadows across the track, and by the time we reached the trading post the light of hurricane lamps from the stalls dimly lit the faces of the crowd gathered in the road. Lturungen felt revived from his rest and from the coolness of the night air, and he led me along to the Roman Catholic compound, the only establishment boasting electricity. The illuminated cross on the church tower picked out in red light bulbs looked a misplaced and tawdry representation of contemporary city life in a setting not far removed from the Iron Age.

It was Saturday evening, and numbers of young people were heading for the community hall to watch a video. The place was crowded. Lturungen was unimpressed with the show and so instead we went on a tour of the primary school buildings. Like so many rural schools, the windows lacked glass. In one poorly lit classroom groups of boys were busy at their studies. The number of boarders had dwindled significantly since Lturungen had been at the school. We looked in at the dormitory with its vast sea of concrete floor and half a dozen bunk beds scattered across it at all angles like abandoned wrecks. The refectory, too, was bare in the extreme. A roof, walls, unglazed windows and ancient benches and tables.

Nowhere were there the trimmings of European schools — no pictures, plants, decorations, and hardly any books. The buildings were just the bare bones with no flesh on them, and yet when I returned to the school early on the following Monday it was bursting with vitality. Children from a variety of tribes and of all ages had trudged in from miles around. Most were carrying firewood for the school kitchens which they had dutifully collected on the way. As they assembled in the parade ground, I noticed a number of them held out their hands while a teacher passed down each line rapping the out-stretched knuckles with a cane. This mass punishment seemed barbaric.

"Why is he doing this?" I asked Lturungen.

"Those are the ones who didn't bother to collect firewood. That is their punishment," he replied.

Outside the office three young offenders were kneeling on the floor, their bodies frozen into contorted shapes. The headmaster kept his eye on them through the open door as he marked papers on his desk. After a while they were permitted to readjust their positions to relieve their aching limbs. How long they were to stay there I could not imagine. Here was discipline of a different order — not the communal yet rigorous *nkanyit* of the Samburu in which everyone shared — but one which was imposed on those in adversity.

For all that, the children were full of spirit. The flag was hoisted and the national anthem sung with vigour. In class children listened to their teachers with rapt attention and made copious notes — for with so few books to refer to, their memory and their notebooks were all they had to rely upon. The more advanced classes were taught in English and as ever I marvelled at the ease with which these children seemed to master not only their own language, but Swahili and English as well. It seemed deplorable that after displaying so much enthusiasm and industry, the vast majority of these youngsters would never proceed to secondary education. Their parents could not afford the fees.

School boarders received very little supervision after school hours, and on that Saturday evening as we walked round the half-darkened school I wondered who would take charge if a fight broke out, or one of the youngsters suffered a serious accident. We left the Catholic compound and headed back to the main road.

We hadn't eaten since midday, and so we collected Lpiritian from the bar and made our way to one of the roadside shacks euphemistically called 'Hotel Neserian' for a dish of cabbage, rice and meat and cups of tea. The establishment was lit by a single Tilley lamp. Two or three groups of young men sat at the tables as did the landlord, a Turkana in a state of inebriation, who repeated to the assembled company over and over again in a slurring voice that he was 'king of the world'. The conversation was desultory, Lturungen and Lpiritian contributing from our table in a mixture of Swahili and Maa while I kept a judicious silence. When we had eaten the boys went out to join their friends while I went back to our room to read. It was an indication of the quality of our relationship that, while we enjoyed each other's company, we could nevertheless retain our independence and felt free to occupy ourselves as we wanted without in any way impeding each other.

There is a world of difference between the start of the plains less than half a mile away and the climate at Archer's Post. Here the river induced a steamy heat in its gentle valley, made worse inside the buildings because a universal adoption of corrugated iron as a roofing material lacked the insulating properties of the mud and dung used to roof the *ngajijik*. In the moist heat flies were a pest in the daytime, and mosquitos a legion at night. Fortunately I had borrowed a mosquito net in Nairobi.

A less fortunate guest a few rooms away had not taken the same precaution. Infuriated by the intruders and cursing them as he did so, he took up a shoe and bashed away at them for an hour and a quarter. Walls, floor and furniture were all subject to his attack. His rage was such that he was oblivious of the disturbance he caused everyone else on our side of the courtyard, for the walls between the cubicles were only seven foot high and did not reach to the ceiling. The poor chap must have been utterly exhausted by the time he finished, and it says something of the indulgence of the other guests that none took him to task for the disturbance he caused.

Outside in the courtyard the radio blared uncompromisingly, and fell silent only when transmission ceased. Lpiritian and I crammed into our tiny bed under the protection of the single mosquito net. The heat was stifling, and we sweated profusely. I longed for the peace and freedom of the *ngajii*. In spite of it all I slept deeply, waking only once to the throbbing vibration of a large truck which halted for a while on the road outside until, all too early, the radio blared again as broadcasts were resumed.

Lpiritian had fared less well. His side of the bed was infested with what looked like bedbugs, and he was badly bitten around the middle. In the circumstances anyone would have been annoyed, but the situation deeply offended Samburu standards of personal hygiene. After we had washed Lpiritian summoned the maid politely but firmly, brought her to the bed and solemnly pulled back the bottom sheet to reveal the cause of his discomfort. His bearing, his blackness of skin and his size compared with the little Meru girl was intimidating.

She was flustered by his coolness and rushed out of the room, to come scurrying back with a tin of powder which she sprinkled liberally over the mattress. Lpiritian watched as she replaced the sheet and nodded his approval. The maid uttered a few hasty words of apology and was gone.

"At three hundred shillings a night I expect something better than this," Lpiritian said with deliberation.

We breakfasted off *mandazis* and sweet warm tea in the little café adjoining the lodgings. It looked seedy in the extreme, and at this hour on a Sunday morning the staff were surly. As time went on we grew concerned for Lturungen. He had not emerged from his bedroom and I knew he wanted to attend church. Eventually we knocked at his door. I was shocked by the room in which we found him. Little better than a chicken shed, it had a timber frame, a low corrugated iron roof and the walls were a pastiche of chicken wire, flattened tin cans, rag and boarding. The mattress on which he slept was filthy, and the mosquito net he had borrowed was full of holes. His foot had been painful all night and he looked utterly exhausted. The sight of Lturungen and his surroundings upset me. What unimaginable force of fate was it which condemned so noble an individual to such pain and squalor?

It was something of a special day for the Roman Catholics in Archer's Post because three new priests were to be introduced to the parishioners. The vaguely Italianate interior of the church and the resplendent robes of the priests and servers contrasted strongly with the poverty and squalor outside. Poor though the congregation may have been in material terms, it was nevertheless blessed by the richness of its singing. Singing has always taken precedence over instrumental music for the peoples of East Africa, and the power and intensity of the Swahili choir and the drumming which accompanied it was magnificent. Not to be outdone, there was also a Samburu choir of mainly women in all their finery. This was a Catholic service with a difference, considerable concessions being made to Samburu beliefs. Even when the new priests were introduced to the congregation they were blessed in the traditional Samburu manner with fire, water and wood. When I expressed my surprise later to a Quaker from the west of Kenya, he maintained that what I had witnessed was merely the Roman

Catholic way of ensnaring the tribespeople into their faith, but I believed I knew the Samburu better than that.

How could a people readily embrace rituals based upon a culture totally alien to them, and religious concepts of which they could have little appreciation? Lturungen was nominally a Roman Catholic from his schooldays. I knew his attendance in church and the inspiration he drew from communal worship was important to him. It was a matter we had discussed on several occasions. Nevertheless it was only an adjunct to his unshakeable belief in Nkai and the spirituality of all life. Sitting next to a window, as the voices of the congregation swelled in praise, I looked out at the shimmering Doum palms standing head and shoulders above the other trees as they marked out the course of the river. Silently I added my praise for having had my eyes opened to a richer, deeper understanding of life and its values, by these nomadic people.

After the service the owner of the Hotel Neserian, suitably sober for a Sunday morning, nodded a greeting as he passed and Amos came up and spoke to us.

"Why don't you take him to the Anglican church?" he said to Lturungen.

"Won't the service be over now?"

"Not at all. He preaches such a long sermon the congregation will still be there."

We walked across the road, down the embankment and arrived at the door of a tiny ramshackle wooden church. We went in. Sure enough, the sermon was still in progress. The Reverend Peter Kamaro looked up from his notes, greeted us in English, informed us of the text for his sermon and continued preaching in Swahili. The congregation numbered about two dozen instead of the four hundred across the road, and was made up of mainly women and rather restless children. Almost all were Samburu. There was also a lone chicken which wandered round the church with the air of authority of a sidesman. There was none of the splendour of the Roman Catholic establishment; merely a cross made of two sticks standing on a rough wooden altar and a roughly hewn lectern. When the sermon finished the congregation sang lustily to the accompaniment of a single drum — in their tribal language which pleased Lturungen hugely. Afterwards everyone assembled outside while I took a photograph.

The heat made Lturungen's foot painful. After lunch the three of us headed to the one cool spot, down by the river under the span of the road bridge. When he was living in Archer's Post it was here that Lturungen came day after day to rest his foot, sitting in the framework of girders which spanned the river. On this particular afternoon Lturungen sat writing letters to the friends he had made in England and which I was to take back with me to save him postage.

Friends came and went, stopping to pass the time of day. One individual, who had more to impart than most, settled down where the bank rose to meet the inside of the bridge and kept up a stream of conversation with the staccato-like words of his native language reverberating amongst the steel and concrete supports. Every now and then Lturungen grunted in reply and turned over a new page in his notepad. Nothing would deflect him from his letter-writing. It took his whole concentration to prise words from a brain numbed by the pain of his foot.

Lpiritian stretched himself out on the concrete footing next to the river and was soon snoring sonorously, and later awoke and waded into the river which was only thigh deep. He stripped and washed on the far bank. Other young boys and a few warriors came down to wash as well, each of them distancing themselves from the bridge by about 100 yards, a measure which they evidently deemed sufficient to maintain their modesty from the prying eyes of the few locals in the vicinity and the occasional vanload of tourists which passed on the road above.

When he had finished washing and returned to our side of the bank, Lpiritian signalled to me to follow him down the river. A couple of younger boys joined us. We walked on loose wet sand for part of the way, splashing along the edge of the water. Then almost without warning, the rocks closed in on either side and the river entered a ravine. Ahead of us the river swung into a sharp left-hand bend. We departed from its main course and climbed up on to sun-bleached rocks to our left. Some of them had been made smooth by the force of water and they served as an overflow when the river was in flood. Now we found ourselves in a different world. Great slabs of rock rose into the clear blue sky. Bushes and small trees found a footing wherever they could, green and succulent from the moist air rising from the river.

It contrasted strangely with the dried and dusty plains all around. We sat and watched crocodiles sunning themselves on the rocks below and then descended to water level to follow the river downstream as it coursed through rapids and cascaded over one waterfall after another. The torrent was the colour of milk chocolate and contrasted strangely with the sun bleached rocks on either side.

Lpiritian led the way. I was touched by the courtesy of the two young boys who, although they hardly knew me, hung back as I jumped from boulder to boulder, ready to offer a steadying hand in case I slipped. We rested on a sandy beach. The boys dug a hollow in the sand and waited for clear water to seep through from the river and then knelt and drank. Cliffs rose on the opposite bank, deeply scoured at their base by flood water. Some warriors came out of a cave in the cliff and exchanged greetings across the river, shouting above the roar of the water. Further on the rocks fell away, the banks flattened out and round a bend we surprised a mother and daughter washing clothes in the river. Lpiritian led us up the bank into scrubland and paused.

"You will never guess what was here!" he exclaimed.

I looked around and on a bluff, rising above the bushes and commanding a view back to Archer's Post, was the remains of a stone home, now roofless and decayed.

"This was Mr Archer's house," Lpiritian said triumphantly. "And over here was the meat factory controlled by him."

A hundred yards from the house lay the foundations of what had been a substantial building. It seemed remarkable that such a large enterprise could have been built in a part of Kenya which in 1910 was at the back of beyond and where roads were no more than tracks through the bush. Such a large expanse of concrete flooring and cast iron supports seemed incongruous. All the other older buildings in the vicinity are constructed of easily portable corrugated iron and wood.

Geoffrey Archer had been sent to the Northern Frontier District in 1909 by the government to regulate the activities of armed and indiscriminate meat traders who procured meat from tribesmen in exchange for cloth, copper wire and beads. The meat processing plant set up on this site operated successfully for a number of years. Then the management decided to slaughter a camel which had been in service since the beginning of the enterprise. The creature had outlived its useful life. Some of the employees were attached to the animal and were reluctant to see its demise. When it was about to be slaughtered the camel raised its head and spoke.

"Why do you want to end my life? I have been a good and faithful servant all these years. I have been your beast of burden and I have provided you with milk," it said. "Do I deserve to be slaughtered just because I have grown old?"

At that the employees panicked. They picked up their belongings and fled. Production was never resumed.

Lturungen continued his letter-writing while Lpiritian and I went back to the shops in search of tea and *uji*, which is a kind of gruel. In the cool of the late afternoon he and I struck out in a north-easterly direction along a path which climbed gently out of the valley and afforded us spectacular views of the surrounding hills. There, in the fresher air on the edge of the plains but just within sight of Archer's Post, we came to a sizeable *nkang* belonging to the younger brother of the eldest of Lpiritian's father's four wives. All the people living there seemed elderly, but that did not mean we were made any less welcome.

I was treated as if I had been a long-lost relative and we sat on stools with the menfolk in a circle under a tree in the gathering dusk. Mugs were passed around, each of which had been filled with Samburu 'whisky' from an old tin can. The air was buzzing with flies, and I watched as they fought each other for a space on the rim of the mug which had been handed to me. As I lifted it to my lips they departed in a swarm. The liquid inside was dark and sweet, and had been made from fermented honey and herbs. I reckoned the alcoholic content to be relatively low, and by the time I had downed the second mugful the effects were negligible. The women had retreated into the huts on our arrival and now came with freshly made tea served in grubby glass tumblers. Our departure was marked with copious handshakes, and I could see from their attitude that these elders held Lpiritian in high esteem.

On the way back we met up with Lturungen. He had finished his letter-writing but had left it too late to get anything to eat. Every single hotel and café had run out of food. There would be nothing more to eat until fresh supplies arrived the following day!

CHAPTER THIRTEEN

Farewell — *Lesere*

WITHOUT PERSONAL transport, travelling to and from Archer's Post is far from easy. There was a scheduled bus to Isiolo, the nearest town, every other day but it was far from reliable and often did not turn up at all. I could have tried to hitch a lift in a passing vehicle, but these were few and far between. The only sure way of reaching Isiolo, and thence the regular bus service to Nairobi, was to walk the twenty-odd miles — and that certainty was tempered by the possibility of being attacked by bandits on the way.

Acknowledging all these difficulties, I arranged to fly back to Nairobi from the Samburu airstrip. I had assumed, and not without good reason, that an airstrip frequented by regular internal flights would be easily accessible to intending passengers. In fact the runway is inside the Samburu National Reserve through which no one is allowed to go on foot, and no public transport is available. It seemed that all passengers to the Samburu area stayed at one or other of the safari lodges and were transported to and fro from them in the safety of safari vehicles.

The one and only taxi owner in Archer's Post was out of town, and the only other vehicle available was that belonging to the General Stores. There was no chance of catching the flight unless the owner could be persuaded to allow his vehicle to be used. If I missed the aeroplane I might find myself trapped in northern Kenya for several days. Lturungen and Lpiritian decided the only thing to do was for them to negotiate the best deal they could with the store owner.

An astute man, he realised the predicament I was in and knew he had me over a barrel. The sum he demanded was a king's ransom and more than I had in cash. Thinking I might yet outflank him I asked if he would accept a Visa card.

"Of course I can, but there will be an additional service charge."

Who would have thought anyone in this place would have had the means of accepting a credit card. But this man was Mr Archer's Post. He ran the only comprehensively stocked store in the place. Every basic food and hardware requirement of the resident and itinerant population was met.

An imposing figure, he sat at a large desk just inside the store and from this commanding position kept a wary eye on his customers and the staff alike. It seemed there was nothing he did not know about the goings-on in the trading post, and I reckoned he knew my need even before the boys approached him. I reluctantly handed over my card and the twenty minute journey to the airstrip was secured.

There seems to be an unwritten law in Kenya, and most likely elsewhere in Africa, that commissioning a vehicle does not confer upon one sole occupancy unless it be a self-drive arrangement. When the time came to set off there were at least five others waiting to travel in the van as well. As procurer of the vehicle I was, however, accorded the privilege of sitting on the bench seat in the front along with Lturungen and the driver, while the others piled into the goods area behind.

Among them was Francis, another Samburu. He had suffered polio as a youngster and walked with a severe limp. I learned that he had been at secondary school with Lturungen, but having acquired his disablement later in life and spared the pain which so dogged Lturungen, he had succeeded in taking a course in accounting and was now cashier to the Samburu Game Lodge at Larsen's Camp. Francis engaged in cheerful banter, requesting me to find an eligible wife for him in England and speculating on the kind of girl I would choose. The others joined in the ribaldry, and the vehicle resounded with laughter. Lturungen, however, remained silent. I was aware that our parting was going to be a tough occasion for him.

We had an hour to spare before the plane arrived. It seemed that we had set out early so that Francis and the others who joined us on the journey should arrive at the Safari Lodge in time for work. The driver of the vehicle decided to while away the time by driving round the reserve, and the others were enjoying themselves so much that notwithstanding their duties they decided to remain with us. No doubt the blame could be placed on my shoulders because I would be safely away from the Samburu District before they started work. I was especially glad to have a look around the reserve as it was one I had not visited before. As I anticipated, the area was full of animals drawn there by the plentiful water supplies which were denied them out in the plains. It was like a giant open-air zoo, and we must have seen fifteen or more different species in the time available to us.

The airstrip was in the middle of nowhere, surrounded by bush. Its only features were a crumbling white tower which had no function as far as I could see, a latrine enclosed in a small wooden shed and a single bench with a wooden awning as protection from the sun. We got out of the van and waited. Eventually a dot appeared in the sky, grew larger, took on the form of a small twin-engined aeroplane and landed. A few tourists were driven onto the concrete runway and we followed on foot. The brothers had now fallen silent. There were handshakes all round. It would have been unthinkable for Lpiritian and Lturungen to have expressed emotion in front of their fellow tribesmen, yet I was aware from the intensity of their handshakes that they regarded this as more than a usual parting. I shared with them the feeling of the coming separation. Within minutes we were airborne, and circling the vehicles on the ground below us. I had expected them to drive off immediately, but the white van which had transported us remained where it was parked until distance obscured it from view.

Mondays are not busy days for up-country flights. There were only six of us on board and the pilot had no other passengers to pick up en route. Far below I caught sight of the Wuaso Ngiro for the last time, and here and there a *nkang*, the surrounding thorn stockade clearly visible on the barren ground to the south of the river. We had time to spare, and the pilot decided to enhance our journey by deviating from his scheduled route to fly past the twin peaks of Mount Kenya. The arid Samburu plains gave way to greener pastures, and as we climbed so the vegetation grew thicker and more lush until we were flying over densely forested land. Then came the rocky slopes of this equatorial mountain giant and finally we rushed up towards the peaks, the snowfields sparkling in the crystal-clear air. At this time of the day the mountain is clear of cloud and stands gaunt against the blue backdrop. Surpassed in Africa only by its close brother Kilimanjaro, to see it in all its grandeur from such close quarters was both exhilarating and breathtaking.

Kenya is a land of contrast. Tribesmen's cattle die for lack of pasture while, looking down on them locked in ice and snow, is all the water they could ever want. There is the marvel of aviation too while, below, souls rub two sticks together to light fires.

The aircraft swung towards Nairobi and before long we were crossing the corrugated hills and valleys which lie like so much pleating to the north of the city. As we came in to land, flying low over the freedom monument, I experienced for a moment the same kind of doubt and depression Lturungen must have experienced on the flight to England. He had faced the uncertainty of an unknown land and the constraints which those in authority imposed upon his endeavours. In my case an experience so overwhelming and so fundamental caused me to doubt my ability to resume a life bound by business and financial pressures, a rigid timescale and the haste and impetuousness of everyday living. How much of the quality and values of life I had come to appreciate in the bush could I cling to — even put into practice — when once again I reached home?

That evening in Nairobi I sat on my bed and prepared myself for a bath, and then to pack for the journey to England. I unlaced my shoes and took off my socks. I blinked hard. Both the socks and shoes had partially disappeared from view.

At first I thought I must be suffering from a touch of sunstroke since it can affect one's sight in this way. Then I realised a small cloud of very fine dust was suspended in the stillness of the bedroom. Slowly, very slowly it dispersed and settled and the socks and shoes came back into view. Before leaving Archer's Post, I had washed thoroughly and put on clean clothes for the journey back. Even so, the all-pervading dust of Samburuland had reasserted itself during the few steps I had taken across the road and into the van, clinging irrepressibly to my footwear.

I sensed it would never let go of me, and I knew that before long I would return.

Lturungen in Thurloxton Church, England

LIST OF CHARACTERS

LPIRITIAN'S MOTHER	Second wife of Lpiritian's father. Five surviving children, namely: Lpiritian, Buni, Lturungen, Ngalina and Karaito.
LPIRITIAN	Eldest son and head of the family since the death of his father. Married to Morissa with one son, Alberto.
BUNI	Second son. Married to Nasaba. No children.
LTURUNGEN	Third son. Unmarried.
NGALINA	Only daughter. Widowed at age sixteen. No children. Looks after Lmunyaki, her half brother.
KARAITO	Fourth son. Circumcised January 1994, aged about twelve.
LITTLE MOTHER	Third wife of Lpiritian's father. Mother of Lobuka and Lmunyaki.
LMUNYAKI	Half brother of Lturungen
LOBUKA	Elder brother of Lmunyaki and half brother of Karaito. Circumcised January 1994 aged about twelve.
SENENE	Half brother of Lpiritian by his father's first wife.
ISAAC	Friend of Lturungen.
JONATHAN and LONGOLOTO	Warriors initiated with the 1990 Lmooli age-set. From February 1994 guardians of Karaito and Lobuka. Jonathan is brother to Nasaba, Buni's wife.
LEKALAILE and LERANTILEI	Junior elders. Sponsors to Karaito at his circumcision.
AMOS	Age-mate of Lpiritian, living in Archer's Post.
FRANCIS	Friend and school mate of Lturungen.

GLOSSARY

AARE	Two
DOINYO	Mountain (Maasai)
ESERIAN	Hello (to several children or married women)
ILE	Six
IMET	Five
ISEAT	Eight
JAMBO	Hello (Swahili)
LAIBARTAK	The name for boys in the period between circumcision and warriorhood
LAIS (plural LAISI)	One specialising in finding lost property by divination
LAJII	Age-set
LAKITONI	Circumciser
LALEM (plural LALEMA)	Short or long sword
LBAAN	Dried riverbed
LEBARTA	Song of circumcision
LKIYAA LOLTOMIA	Ivory earrings
LMUGET LOOLBAA	Ceremony of the arrows. The first of five ceremonies marking the passage of warriorhood
LMURRAN (singular LMURRANI)	Samburu warriors
LMINONG	Ceremony permitting a man to eat and drink for the first time in the presence of his wife
LOIKOP	The Samburu name for their tribe, Samburu being a name of Maasai origin

LORORA	A circular encampment of huts surrounded by a thorn 'hedge' or fence, specially constructed for circumcision and warrior-making ceremonies
LPAYIAN	Husband or married man
LTULELEI	A plant used to make a lethal poison, effective in killing elephants and people
LUYHA	Bantu tribe from western Kenya
MAA	The language common to the Maasai and Samburu
MANDAZI	Triangular doughnut (Swahili)
MPARATUT	Wife
MPORRO	Necklace worn by married women
MURRATA	One who is circumcised
MURATARE	Circumcision
MZUNGU (plural WAZUNGU)	White man (Swahili)
NAAPO	Open space in the centre of the LORORA (qv) where elders assemble to discuss business
NABO	One
NANGA	Cloth wrap to cover the body
NCHIPI	Blue or blue and white beads and beetle wing cases worn by boys awaiting circumcision
NDAA	Food
NDOKUNA	Fit, usually brought on by stress, more common in men than women
NGAJII (plural NGAJIJIK)	Samburu dwelling
NGERAI	Children
NGUARIYE	Night
NJILII	Ornament in the form of a pyramidal cross commonly worn by Samburu warriors and women on their foreheads
NKAI	God

NKANG (plural NKANGITE)	Samburu encampment	
NKANYIT	Discipline, often associated with honour and respect	
NKARE	Water	
NKIKE	Toothbrush stick	
NKIYEU	Name used by a warrior and his guardian, after the roasted fat used as a symbol of kinship	
OONGWAN	Four	
POSHO	Maize porridge (Swahili)	
RUNGU	Stick with a club head (Swahili)	
SAAL	Nine	
SAPA	Seven	
SEKOTEI	Samburu name for the tree from which toothbrush sticks are made *(Salvadora persica)*	
SERECHOI	A tree whose wood, when burnt, is used as a milk preservative	
SHIFTA	Armed Somali bandits (Swahili)	
SILALEI	Gum from *Boswellia neglecta* (Commiphora family) used to tip the arrows of newly circumcised boys	
SINTANI	A name used between sisters-in-law	
SIRAN	Morning	
SUPA!	Samburu greeting	
TOMON	Ten	
UJI	Gruel (Swahili)	
UUNI	Three	
WATOTO	Children (Swahili)	
WAZUNGU	see MZUNGU	

Other publications in Scriptmate Editions'
'People in their Places' series:

Shooting Star—The Last of the Silent Film Stars by Chili Bouchier. The frank memories of Britain's first 'IT' Girl. Over 80 pictures, including three 8-page plate sections illustrating seven decades of theatre and film. 272pp. ISBN 0-9513766-6-7

Echoes from the Land by Ann Kritzinger. Based on historical fact, this novel about a young girl's frontier legacy contested by ruthless men exposes the horrors and betrayals of South Africa's race struggle of the early 1800s. 216pp. ISBN 0-9513766-7-5